AA

50 Walks in
DORSET

This book is dedicated to the memory of Skipper (1988–2002),
a Jack Russell of great character, who loved these walks.

First published 2002
Researched and written by Ann F Stonehouse

Produced by AA Publishing
© Automobile Association Developments Limited 2002
Illustrations © Automobile Association Developments Limited 2002

Published by AA Publishing (a trading name of Automobile
Association Developments Limited, whose registered office is
Millstream, Maidenhead, Windsor, SL4 5GD;
registered number 1878835). A00905

Ordnance Survey® This product includes mapping data licensed from
Ordnance Survey® with the permission of the
Controller of Her Majesty's Stationery Office. © Crown copyright
2002. All rights reserved. Licence number 399221.

ISBN 0 7495 3338 2

A CIP catalogue record for this book is available
from the British Library.

The contents of this book are believed correct at the time of printing.
Nevertheless, the publishers cannot be held responsible for any errors
or omissions or for changes in the details given in this book or for
the consequences of any reliance on the information it provides. We
have tried to ensure accuracy in this book, but things do change and
we would be grateful if readers would advise us of any inaccuracies
they may encounter.

We have taken all reasonable steps to ensure that these walks are
safe and achievable by walkers with a realistic level of fitness.
However, all outdoor activities involve a degree of risk and the
publishers accept no responsibility for any injuries caused to
readers whilst following these walks. For more advice on walking
safely see page 128. The mileage range shown on the front cover is for
guidance only – some walks may exceed or be less than these
distances.

Visit the AA Publishing website at www.theAA.com

Paste-up and editorial by Outcrop Publishing Services Ltd, Cumbria
for AA Publishing

Colour reproduction by LC Repro
Printed in Italy by G Canale & C SPA, Torino, Italy

Legend

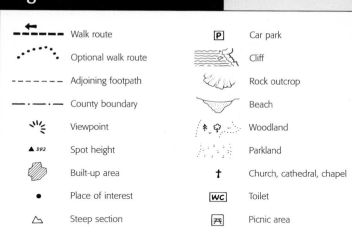

⬅ - - - - -	Walk route	P	Car park
••••••••	Optional walk route		Cliff
- - - - - -	Adjoining footpath		Rock outcrop
—·—·—·—	County boundary		Beach
☀	Viewpoint	♠ ♀	Woodland
▲ 392	Spot height		Parkland
⬗	Built-up area	†	Church, cathedral, chapel
●	Place of interest	WC	Toilet
△	Steep section	🎪	Picnic area

Dorset locator map

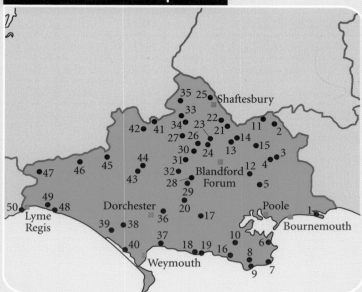

Shaftesbury

35 25
33
42 41 34 23 22 11 2
27 26 21 14
30 24 13 15 3
44 31 12 4
47 46 45 32 Blandford 5
43 28 Forum
29
49 Dorchester 20 17 Poole 1
50 48 36 Bournemouth
Lyme 39 38 10
Regis 37 6
40 18 19 16 8
Weymouth 9 7

Contents

Contents

Rating: Each walk is rated for its relative difficulty compared to the other walks in this book. Walks marked 🚶 🚶 🚶 are likely to be shorter and easier with little total ascent. The hardest walks are marked 🚶 🚶 🚶 .

Walking in Safety: For advice and safety tips ➤ 128.

Introducing Dorset

A dark diamond of green velvet on the patchwork quilt of English counties is how I used to imagine Dorset. My first visit was a teenage literary pilgrimage to Lyme Regis (well, Jane Austen for me and fossils for my brother). We stayed in a nautical B&B and ate fish and chips in a sharp wind out on the Cobb, while pretending to be Meryl Streep. I loved it. It was a revelation and I've been enjoying a wider discovery of Dorset ever since.

Be warned: as the good people of Dorset know only too well, there is no point in visiting their county in a hurry. There are no motorways here, and the trunk roads, bold enough on the map, are invariably shared with tractors, tanks, cows and holiday caravans. So relax and slow down. Better still, prepare to leave your car and start exploring on foot, for that's when you'll see the best of the hidden valleys and secretive hamlets that the county has to offer.

And the walking in Dorset is great. With the exception of some of the more spectacular cliffs along the coast, it's rarely strenuous and you're unlikely to get lost for long. There are no vast moorland wastes, scary mountains or devilish quicksands here. Folk have been tramping over Dorset since time immemorial and have left behind them an intricate network of lanes and byways, broad green droving roads and bridlepaths, which today is blessedly well-signposted. You'll find yourself criss-crossing long distance trails such as the Wessex Ridgeway, the Thomas Hardy Way, the Monarch's Way and the Liberty Trail. And finding your place on the map is not difficult in a landscape where there's generally a little farmhouse or two somewhere in sight, or a lichened church tower to announce the next village.

With the exception of the unlovely urban spread that is Bournemouth and Poole rolled into one, the towns here are mostly small and full of character. Lyme Regis, Shaftesbury and Dorchester form a useful trinity of centres, each in a different world.

In the south west corner, near the Somerset border, Lyme is a seaside holiday town, its historic heart the familiar backdrop to many a celluloid tale of sailing ships. It offers unrivalled access to Dorset's western coast, with its pretty little villages, its crumbly golden cliffs and the remarkable long shingle strand that is Chesil Beach.

Shaftesbury, at the northern point of the Dorset diamond, is a bustling market town set on a high hill, the key to the chalky sweep of Cranborne Chase and the fertile flats of the Blackmoor Vale. The roads from here

---

PUBLIC TRANSPORT ⓘ

In a predominantly rural county like Dorset, public transport options are limited. With that in mind, all these walks are circular, allowing you to return to a start point and vehicle. For details of public transport services across the county, ring the national inquiry service on 0870 6082608; it's open daily from 7AM to 8PM. You can also find bus and rail information on the internet at www.pti.org.uk.

wind gently south towards Wareham and the shallow fingers of Poole Harbour, and south east to the historic centres of Wimborne Minster and Christchurch.

Dorchester lies inland from the southern tip of the diamond, an access hub for the green centre of the county, with roads leading south to Weymouth and the Isle of Portland, west to Bridport, north along the lovely Cerne Valley, and east to the white cliffs of the Isle of Purbeck and beyond. The stately town is synonymous with the name of the Victorian novelist and poet, Thomas Hardy, who immortalised a still recognisable Dorsetshire landscape.

Wherever you walk, you'll find that the hills, hedgerows and coastline are teeming with deer, birds and other wildlife. It's worth carrying binoculars with you and being prepared to stop and watch patiently – the wildlife will invariably come to you. There are so many great possibilities for walkers all around Dorset that couldn't be crammed in here. Look on this selection as the first 50, and enjoy the further discovery yourselves.

Using this Book

Information panels
An information panel for each walk shows its relative difficulty (➤ 5), the distance and total amount of ascent. An indication of the gradients you will encounter is shown by the rating ▲▲ ▲▲ ▲▲ (no steep slopes) to ▲▲ ▲▲ ▲▲ (several very steep slopes).

Maps
There are 30 maps, covering 40 of the walks. Some walks have a suggested option in the same area. The information panel for these walks will tell you how much extra walking is involved. On short-cut suggestions the panel will tell you the total distance if you set out from the start of the main walk. Where an option returns to the same point on the main walk, just the distance of the loop is given. Where an option leaves the main walk at one point and returns to it at another, then the distance shown is for the whole walk. The minimum time suggested is for reasonably fit walkers and doesn't allow for stops. Each walk has a suggested map. Laminated aqua3 maps are longer lasting and water resistant.

Start Points
The start of each walk is given as a six-figure grid reference prefixed by two letters indicating which 100km square of the National Grid it refers to. You'll find more information on grid references on most Ordnance Survey maps.

Dogs
We have tried to give dog owners useful advice about how dog friendly each walk is. Please respect other countryside users. Keep your dog under control, especially around livestock, and obey local bylaws and other dog control notices.

Car Parking
Many of the car parks suggested are public, but occasionally you may find you have to park on the roadside or in a lay-by. Please be considerate when you leave your car, ensuring that access roads or gates are not blocked and that other vehicles can pass safely.

Heights and Huts of Hengistbury Head

An easy coastal loop with much to see.

•DISTANCE•	3¼ miles (5.3km)
•MINIMUM TIME•	2hrs
•ASCENT / GRADIENT•	109ft (33m) ▲ ▲ ▲
•LEVEL OF DIFFICULTY•	👣 👣 👣
•PATHS•	Grass, tarmac road, soft sand, woodland track, some steps
•LANDSCAPE•	Heathland, sand cliffs, sand spit, mixed woodland
•SUGGESTED MAP•	aqua3 OS Explorer OL 22 New Forest
•START / FINISH•	Grid reference: SZ 163912
•DOG FRIENDLINESS•	Keep to paths to avoid destroying habitat and disturbing ground-nesting birds
•PARKING•	Car park (fee) at end of road, signed 'Hengistbury Head' from B3059
•PUBLIC TOILETS•	Beside car park; also amid beach huts

BACKGROUND TO THE WALK

The multi-coloured beach huts of Mudeford's sandy peninsula are a cheerful throwback to nostalgic bucket-and-spade holidays of the early 20th century. In fact, they hark back to the last days of the century before that, when bathers would undress in modest little huts on wheels, which could be horse-hauled down into the shallows in order to minimise any embarrassing exposure to public view.

Huts of Fashion

With the quantities of flesh readily flashed in this modern era (➤ Walk 6), those days are long gone, but the carriages' successors, the huts, are still there and the desire for one's own bit of space right on the beach remains undiminished. In the fashion of the day, candy-striped paintwork has given way to bold, plain colours, but the urge to individualise remains strong, with decks, weathervanes and windmilling, semaphoring sailors.

While the huts' outer form remains much the same – central door, symmetrical windows, shallow, peaked roof – the insides are a Nosy Parker's dream. Some make the most of one light, airy space reflecting sparkling sea and sky, others may be divided into rooms, with perhaps a sleeping platform squeezed up under the roof. Each is customised with its owner's particular beach 'necessities' – minimalist fridge and drinks cabinet in one, kitchen sink and home comforts in another. Names offer a further insight into owners' identities: whimsical Riverdance stands next door to jokey Liverdance, and Tardis and Baywatch reflect the TV generations.

Barn Field

The windswept peninsula of Hengistbury Head has an archaeological record dating back 12,500 years, when Stone-Age hunter-gatherers left the remains of a camp site on its outer, seaward edge. Some 10,500 years later Iron-Age folk settled here and built up a trading port on the more sheltered inner shore, where Barn Field stands today. The great Double Dikes date from this later period, built to shelter a village of timber-framed dwellings.

Barn Field itself has remained untouched by farming improvements since the Romans left around AD 410 – a rare status that is jealously protected by conservationists, especially on this crowded south coast, where land is at a premium. Its vegetation is low, acidic grassland that grips on to thin soil over gravel and sand, maintained down the centuries by salt-laden winds and the sharp teeth of the rabbit population. Decimation of the rabbits in the 1950s by myxomatosis allowed gorse and bramble to gain a hold, but a recent programme of scrub clearance and controlled grazing by cattle, managed by English Nature, has done much to restore the original balance. Today it is an important site for ground-nesting birds such as the skylark and meadow pipit, and adorned with the flowers of heath bedstraw, autumn hawkbit and harebell.

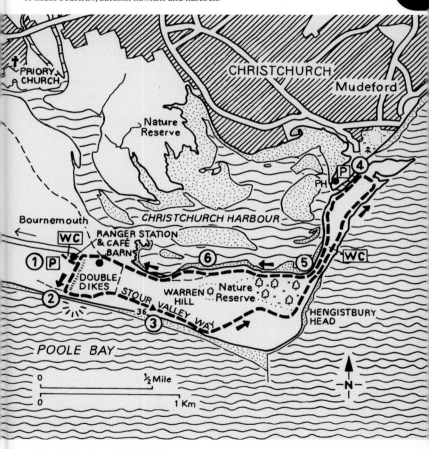

Walk 1 Directions

① From the corner of the car park take the grassy path towards the sea, with the fenced-off lines of the

Double Dikes to your left. At the sea-edge you can see for miles each way: to the towers of Bournemouth, the chalky Foreland and Durlston Head to the west, Christchurch Bay and the Isle of Wight to the east.

Walk 1

② Turn left and follow the road along the cliffs. The Priory Church in Christchurch dominates the view inland across the harbour, with St Catherine's Hill behind. Follow the road up the hill. Pause to admire the boggy pond on your right, home to the rare natterjack toad. The road narrows; climb up some steps, passing a numbered post marking the **Stour Valley Way**. As you climb the steep path, the views back along the coast are fabulous, and there are views across the shallows of Christchurch Harbour, usually buzzing with windsurfers and sailing dinghies.

③ On the heathy top of **Warren Hill** a viewing platform tells you that you're 75 miles (120km) from Cherbourg and 105 miles (168km) from Jersey. Keep right along the path, passing a deserted coastguard station and following the top of the cliffs. Descend into a deep hollow,

where the sea appears to be breaking through. Keep straight on, following the curve of the head, with views across to the Needles. At the end the path turns down through some trees; descend the steps. Walk along the sparkling, white sand on the sea side of the beach huts to the point. Stone groynes form little bays.

④ At the end of the spit you're only a stone's throw from the opposite shore (a ferry runs across to the pub from the end of a pier, passed further on). Turn round the end of the point, passing the old **Black House**, and walk up the inner side of the spit, overlooking the harbour.

⑤ If you've had enough beach and breeze, you can catch the land train back to the car park from here (times vary seasonally). Otherwise, join the metalled road which curves round to the right past the freshwater marsh and lagoon.

⑥ At a post marked '19' turn right on to the sandy path and follow it briefly through the woods, crossing a small ditch, to emerge back on the road. Turn right, passing extensive reedbeds on the right and a **bird sanctuary** on the left. Continue past the thatched barn and follow the road to the **café**, ranger station building and car park.

Down, Ditch and Dyke from Pentridge

A stiff climb leads to a dramatic defensive earthwork.

•DISTANCE•	3½ miles (5.7km)
•MINIMUM TIME•	2hrs
•ASCENT / GRADIENT•	475ft (145m) ▲▲▲
•LEVEL OF DIFFICULTY•	🏃🏃 🏃🏃 🏃🏃
•PATHS•	Steep, muddy farmland, grassy sward, farm roads, 4 stiles
•LANDSCAPE•	Chalk downs, open grassland, fields and copse
•SUGGESTED MAP•	aqua3 OS Explorer 118 Shaftesbury & Cranborne Chase
•START / FINISH•	Grid reference: SU 034178
•DOG FRIENDLINESS•	No problems
•PARKING•	Lay-by in Pentridge or start from car park at Martin Down
•PUBLIC TOILETS•	None on route

BACKGROUND TO THE WALK

At 607ft (185m) high, Penbury Knoll has made a good lookout over Cranborne Chase since settlers first left their mark on this quiet corner of north east Dorset, some 5,000 years ago. The maps show signs of Celtic field systems (associated with the period around 1000 BC) plotted around the lovely green combe of Pentridge Down, though little is revealed to the naked eye. The extraordinary Dorset Cursus starts to the north of here (► Walk 15), and the landscape is littered with lumpy burial mounds, or tumuli, and long barrows, the most visible signs of early settlement. Grim's Ditch marked a Bronze-Age farm boundary, but a more significant defensive earthwork remains from this period, constructed to protect the long-vanished hill fort against invasion from the north east.

Bokerley Dyke

Bokerley Dyke is a broad scar running down the hill. It consists of a high bank and deep ditch, which originally extended for some 3 miles (4.8km). A matter of weeks' work for a JCB, the construction of the dyke must have taken thousands of hours of punishing hard labour. In the 4th century AD it was strengthened and parts of it were re-dug, as by then it formed an important defence on the Roman route along Ackling Dyke to the stronghold at Badbury Rings (► Walk 12), against Saxon invaders. In the 9th century it again formed a vital part of the defence of Dorset – this time from attacks by the Vikings, who were overrunning the Kingdom of Wessex. King Ethelred I was mortally wounded in a fierce battle on Martin Down, on the other side of the dyke, in AD 871. This event left the way open for his younger brother Alfred to claim the throne of Wessex and eventually make a successful peace with the marauding Danes.

Pentridge

There has been a settlement below the hill at Pentridge since at least the recordings of the Domesday survey in the 11th century, when St Rumbold's Church received its first mention. The quiet hamlet of Pentridge is spared the modern invasion of traffic passing through.

Tiled cob walls mix with flint and brick and thatch, and there's a handsome 18th-century barn. Unusually, little Chestnut Cottage, by the turning to the church, has exposed timbers. Unlike busier villages, where houses jostle forward on to the narrow pavements, here they are set back from the single main street, tucked behind hedges and gardens, or in a silent line further up the hill. There's no orange streetlighting here. In the dusk, little squares of golden light appear, unshaded by curtains, evoking memories of Thomas Hardy's obsession in *The Woodlanders* (1887) with lamps and firelight and looking through people's windows to see life played out.

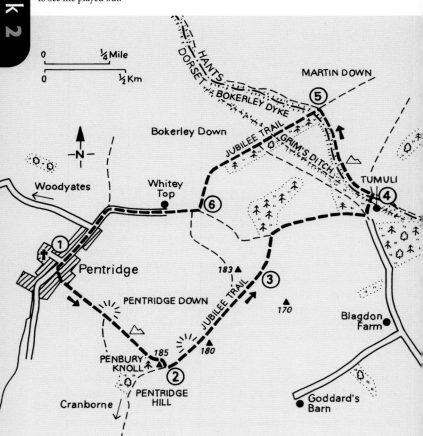

Walk 2 Directions

① From the lay-by walk past the turning up to the church and cross the stile on the left by the footpath sign. Head up the field to a stile, and cross it to enter a narrow footpath. This leads between hedges, straight up the 610ft

(185m) **Pentridge Hill**. Cross another stile into a field and keep straight ahead. As you pause to catch your breath, you can start to admire the view opening around you, with the green curve of Pentridge Down on the left. Keep straight on to the top of the hill (**Penbury Knoll**), passing to the left of a clump of trees.

Walk 2

② At the top turn left on to the **Jubilee Trail** footpath, which runs along the ridge of the down beside an ancient hedge line. (There are fabulous views on either side – Pentridge is largely hidden in the trees.) After ½ mile (800m) the path starts to descend.

WHILE YOU'RE THERE ⓘ

Explore **Martin Down**, on the other side of the Dyke, and just over the border into Hampshire. A National Nature Reserve in the care of English Nature, it consists of open tracts of chalk downland, dotted with wild flowers including purple clover, lilac-coloured scabious and soft blue harebells, with heath, scrub and woodland.

③ Turn right, through a gate into a copse, following the Jubilee Trail marker, and descend along the field edge. Soon bear left across the field to a fingerpost in the hedge, to turn right down a muddy track. There are good views of Bokerley Dyke curving away to your left. Descend through woodland to a gate at the bottom. Go through and turn right, on to a bridleway. Pass a metal gate and immediately hook back left on a chalky track. As you start to descend, curious mounds appear to the right – tumuli.

④ Cross **Grim's Ditch** and **Bokerley Dyke** on to the nature reserve of **Martin Down**, and immediately turn left on to the grassy path, which runs along the east side of the ditch. Follow this downhill for ½ mile (800m).

WHAT TO LOOK FOR ⓘ

St Rumbold's Church was rebuilt in 1855 and is a pleasing, unfussy structure of grey stone and flint. Look out for a plaque inside commemorating one Robert Browning who died in 1746: he was a butler and the great-great-grandfather of the famous Victorian poet of the same name.

⑤ At the crossroads of tracks turn left on to the **Jubilee Trail**, by the fingerpost that announces it's only 90 miles (144km) to Forde Abbey. A nettly path runs up the side of mixed woodland. At the end of the woods go straight ahead, through a gate. Follow the field boundary up to the top and cross the stile.

⑥ Turn right and go through the farm gate into a green lane. **Pentridge Down** emerges to the left, with the village hidden by trees. Pass through another gate on to a farm track between high hedges. Continue down to the bottom and follow it round to the left. Walk back into the village along the main street to return to your car.

Horton's Rebel King

A luscious landscape, where once a rebel was roused.

•DISTANCE•	7½ miles (12.1km)
•MINIMUM TIME•	4hrs
•ASCENT / GRADIENT•	426ft (130m) ▲▲▲
•LEVEL OF DIFFICULTY•	🚶🚶 🚶🚶 🚶
•PATHS•	Field paths, tracks, some road, 15 stiles
•LANDSCAPE•	Gently rolling farmland, mixed woodland
•SUGGESTED MAP•	aqua3 OS Explorer OL 22 New Forest; Explorer 118 Shaftesbury & Cranborne Chase
•START / FINISH•	Grid reference: SU 034072 (on Explorer 118)
•DOG FRIENDLINESS•	On lead on road sections
•PARKING•	Lay-by with phone box, just west of Horton
•PUBLIC TOILETS•	None on route

BACKGROUND TO THE WALK

The countryside around Horton holds a sad reminder of a flamboyant rebel, who was captured here after being discovered asleep in a ditch below an ash tree. On 11 June 1685 James, Duke of Monmouth, the illegitimate son of the late King Charles II, landed from exile in Holland at Lyme Regis (► Walk 50). West Dorset was a base for anti-Catholic Dissenters and on earlier visits the Duke had been warmly greeted with cries of 'God bless the Protestant Duke, and the Devil take the Pope'. He believed he could raise enough support in the West Country to claim the throne from his uncle, the Catholic James II.

Accompanied by a small band of supporters, Monmouth set about recruiting. He announced that he had come to defend the Protestant religion and to deliver the country from the tyranny of James II. Within a few days his following had grown to 4,000. At Taunton Monmouth had himself declared King. On 6 July the rebels clashed with James II's forces at Sedgemoor, across the border in Somerset. The battle was over in 90 minutes, with a loss of 16 of the King's men and some 300 rebels. His ill-equipped army having been routed, the Duke was forced to flee with three followers. He hoped to escape on foot, disguised as a local shepherd, through Dorset to the coast at Poole, where he could board a ship.

However, rewards were posted, and the countryside quickly filled with troops seeking the rebel leader. Two of his companions were caught at Holt the next morning. The Duke and his last companion, a German officer named Buyse, fled across the fields of Horton Heath, but were spotted climbing a hedge by an old lady, Amy Farrant, who told the authorities. Buyse was soon captured and a few hours later militiaman Henry Parkin, while searching beneath an ash tree, discovered another exhausted figure. A search of his pockets disclosed the badge of the Knight of the Garter, golden guineas and recipes for cosmetics, revealing that this was no ordinary shepherd. After a defiant declaration that, given the chance, he would do it all again, Monmouth was taken to London. He was beheaded on 15 July.

The repercussions of the failed rebellion were felt hard in Dorset. The brutal Lord Chief Justice Jeffreys was put in charge of the trials of 312 of Monmouth's supporters in what became known as the 'Bloody Assizes' at Dorchester. Most were transported to the colonies, but 74 were executed, their bodies publicly mutilated and hung on display.

Walk **3**

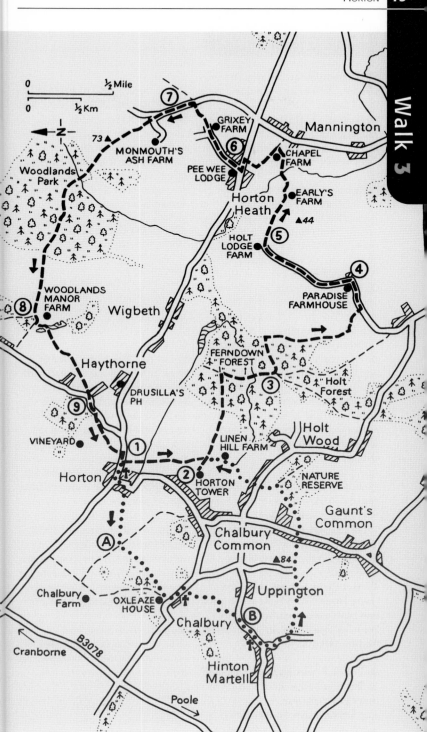

0 ½ Mile
0 ½ Km

N

73 ▲
MONMOUTH'S
ASH FARM

Woodlands
Park

⑦

GRIXEY
FARM
Mannington

⑥
PEE WEE
LODGE
CHAPEL
FARM

Horton
Heath
EARLY'S
FARM
▲44

⑤
HOLT
LODGE
FARM

⑧
WOODLANDS
MANOR
FARM

Wigbeth

④
PARADISE
FARMHOUSE

Haythorne

DRUSILLA'S
PH

FERNDOWN
FOREST

③
Holt
Forest

⑨

VINEYARD

①

LINEN
HILL FARM

Holt
Wood

Horton

②
HORTON
TOWER

NATURE
RESERVE

Gaunt's
Common

Ⓐ

Chalbury
Common
▲84

Uppington

Chalbury
Farm

OXLEAZE
HOUSE

Chalbury

Ⓑ

Cranborne

B3078

Hinton
Martell

Poole

Walk 3 Directions

① Go towards the village and turn left over the stile by the **pump**. Head towards Horton Tower, crossing two more stiles. Go up the hill, bearing diagonally left. Cross the fence at the top corner, and turn right to view the tower.

② Retrace your steps and stay on the track through a gate into **Ferndown Forest.** After ¼ mile (400m) join a firmer track. Shortly, turn right between trees. Cross a stream and a track to a gate.

③ Pass this, go through a bank and turn left along a forest ride. Turn right before the edge of the wood, and follow the path for ¾ mile (1.2km). Bear left at the bottom, down a track. Turn left at the road and pass **Paradise Farmhouse**.

④ Turn left between the houses and follow the road to **Holt Lodge Farm**. With the buildings to your left, bear half-right across the yard to a grassy lane.

⑤ Where this peters out bear left into the field, with the hedge to your right. Cross a stile and go through a gate to **Early's Farm**. Turn immediately left to the gate, and right, in front of the house, into a lane. At a junction after **Chapel Farm**, turn left, signed the 'Long House'. Turn right at the gate and cross a stile. Bear left around the field, cross a stile by a bungalow and another stile to the road.

⑥ Turn left, then right into the lane by **Pee Wee Lodge**. Keep straight on at the junction, then fork right into **Grixey Farm**. Follow the waymarker up the hill, crossing two stiles. With a copse on your left, go up the field. Cross a stile and turn left on to the road.

⑦ After ½ mile (800m) bear left, signed 'Monmouth's Ash Farm', and take the path to the right of the bungalow. Keep straight on this bridleway up over a sandy heath and down into woodland. After a mile (1.6km) the track emerges from the woods, and you can see Horton Tower.

WHERE TO EAT AND DRINK

On the main road east of Horton village is **Drusilla's**, a cosy old pub with a thatched roof, real ales and a fabulous view over to Horton Tower. If you're after a Dorset cream tea, try the **Horton Inn**, at a junction 1 mile (1.6km) west of the village – children and dogs welcome.

---

⑧ Just past **Woodlands Manor Farm** turn left along the road with the fence. Bear down to the right beside the lake and stay on this road. After it becomes a track, look for two stiles in the hedge on the right, just after the farm. Cross these and go diagonally across the field to another stile. Cross the top of the next field and a stile, turning right to meet the road.

⑨ Turn left through **Haythorne** but, before the road descends, go right, through trees, to a gate and down the field, to emerge by the vineyard. Turn left and left again to return to your car.

WHAT TO LOOK FOR

The landmark folly of **Horton Tower** stands like a giant rocket-launcher, splendidly isolated on its hilltop. Some 230ft (70m) high, it was built by Humphrey Sturt in 1762 as an 'observatory', probably for deer-spotting, and was restored in 1994.

Walk 4

A Loop to Chalbury Hill

An extension through pretty villages west of Horton Tower.
See map and information panel for Walk 3

•DISTANCE•	11 miles (17.7km)
•MINIMUM TIME•	6hrs
•ASCENT / GRADIENT•	705ft (215m) ▲▲▲
•LEVEL OF DIFFICULTY•	🚶 🚶 🚶

Walk 4 Directions (Walk 3 option)

An attractive, alternative starting loop can be made through Chalbury Common and Hinton Martell, which has an eccentric, outsize fountain at its centre.

From the lay-by walk into **Horton** and turn left, signed 'Chalbury Common', past the church. Take the path opposite. Cross a stile and follow the path round a barn. Cross a fence and go straight on a track. Cross two stiles and bear right, around the field.

At a junction of tracks by a gateway (Point Ⓐ) turn left across the field towards woods. Cross a stile and bear right to a metal gate. Go through and walk up by the woods. Bear right through a gate and head diagonally up the field. Go through a gate below **Oxleaze House** and up the lane into **Chalbury**. At the road turn left, passing **Chalbury Hill House**. Take the footpath on the right to the church. Leave via the kissing gate and stile opposite the church door, then bear right down the hill. Cross a stile and bear left down the path. Soon cross a stile and footbridge, then cross another stile and follow the path diagonally across the field. Cross a stile and walk between fences. After a further stile the path descends to a track. Turn right and soon left over one more stile, then descend some steps to reach the road at Point Ⓑ.

Turn right and go into **Hinton Martell**. Turn left by the fountain down a lane. When the path rises turn left up a track through woods. Cross a stile and keep straight on, up the field edge. Climb the wooden fence and keep straight on. Bear right at the top corner and follow the field edge to a stile. Walk up to the road, turn left and immediately right down a track. Follow this left and down hill. At the end keep straight ahead on the path and fork right to enter **Holt Wood National Nature Reserve**. After a short distance fork left and keep left along the edge of the wood. At a cross-track turn left – the grassy track meets a gravel road. Follow this between houses to a road. Cross and go up the private road ahead. Continue through a gate, then go on, up to **Linen Hill Farm**. Pass the buildings on your left and cross a stile into a field. Walk straight up to cross a stile into a green lane by **Horton Tower**. Here you can join Walk 34 at Point ②, or walk down the hill to **Horton**.

Wimborne Water-meadows

An easy, level exploration of a historic town and its water-meadows.

•DISTANCE•	4 miles (6.4km)
•MINIMUM TIME•	1hr 30min
•ASCENT / GRADIENT•	Negligible
•LEVEL OF DIFFICULTY•	
•PATHS•	Riverside path (may be muddy), pavement, field paths, lane, 12 stiles
•LANDSCAPE•	Water-meadows to south west and town centre
•SUGGESTED MAP•	aqua3 OS Explorer 118 Shaftesbury & Cranborne Chase
•START / FINISH•	Grid reference: SY 995001
•DOG FRIENDLINESS•	Town walking makes this less than ideal
•PARKING•	Car park on Cowgrove Road beyond football ground
•PUBLIC TOILETS•	Near Minster church

Walk 5 Directions

Walk towards the **River Stour** and turn left, over a stile. Follow the path beside the river for ½ mile (800m), on the **Stour Valley Way**, crossing three more stiles before reaching the football ground, up to your left. This gives way to allotments. The mottled brown towers of the Minster are now seen ahead. The allotment track runs into a little side road. Turn left at the end, towards the town centre, passing through a residential area of

Victorian villas and modern houses – this is **Julians Road**. Emerge opposite the **Pudding and Pye** pub and cross straight over the junction into **West Street**. This winds round past the back of the **King's Head Hotel** into the town's main square. Turn right here, into **Church Street**, passing the **Oddfellows** pub and then toilets on the left, with the Minster straight ahead.

Go straight ahead to visit the **Minster**; its squat, square towers dominate the town centre. The building's foundation dates back to AD 705, when Cuthberga and Cwenburga, sisters to the King of the West Saxons, set up a mixed monastery here. The present building dates from some 400 years later. One of its most fascinating features is the library, founded for the free use of the townspeople in 1686, and consisting of 350 (mainly theological) volumes. To prevent theft of such valuable items, the books were chained to the shelves. The chains were made by orphans in the workhouse.

WHERE TO EAT AND DRINK

You're spoilt for choice in Wimborne. The **Oddfellows**, commended for its garden, offers morning coffee, as well as home-cooked bar food. The **Rising Sun** has a riverside garden and terrace, and offers a tempting selection of sandwiches in ciabatta, pannini and other speciality breads, as well as staples such as jacket potatoes and a children's menu. The historic **Yew Tree Tea Rooms**, dating from 1590, occupy an enviable position overlooking the Minster.

Walk 5

WHILE YOU'RE THERE

Visit the **Priest's House Museum** on the High Street, a medieval house with later additions, originally built for the priests at the Minster but later occupied by various tradespeople, including a printer, a tobacconist and an ironmonger. It's full of the domestic paraphernalia of years gone by, including a Victorian kitchen and a tinsmith's workshop.

After exploring the Minster walk past the **Yew Tree Tea Rooms,** on the left, to meet the **High Street.** Follow this round to the right, to the junction with **King Street** and **East Street.** Turn left here, with a glimpse of the stream on your left. Pass the **Rising Sun** pub on your right, cross the river and keep straight on, picking up Stour Valley Way signs set fairly high on the lamp-posts.

Bear right down **Poole Road.** Pass a large thatched pub, the **Coach and Horses,** on the left, and a stoneware centre on the right. Cross the **River Stour** on a footbridge to one side of the old arched road bridge.

Just for a moment you enter the Borough of Poole. Almost immediately turn right, down a narrow path between houses, signposted 'Lake Gates'. This emerges on to a bungalow estate; follow the green waymarkers straight on through. Next, bear right on another footpath which takes you across the bottom of a children's recreation ground. Cross a stile to continue ahead along a line of trees, above an attractive bend of the river. Turn right over the next stile to walk around the edge of a field, with extensive water-meadows below – look out for cormorants in the river. Cross a stile and turn up left, along the edge of

some woods. Emerge at a lane and turn right (unfortunately, it's noisy from the bypass which runs parallel). Zig-zag under the bypass and go up to a gate.

Go through and along the road, past **Merley Hall farmhouse** on your right. At the end of the lane cross over a road and turn right to reach a roundabout.

WHAT TO LOOK FOR

The Stour supports a rich variety of **wildlife**. Most obvious are the birds, with mallards and mute swans on the water, moorhens, warblers and buntings in the tall reedbeds, and grey herons and exotic white egrets fishing in the shallows. Trout, roach, perch, dace, minnows and eels live in the water, and in summer look out for orange tip, peacock and clouded yellow butterflies, dragonflies and damselflies.

Cross straight over with care and look for the fingerpost pointing into the bushes, signposted 'Stour Valley Way and Pamphill'. Cross the stile and follow a grassy track as it bends to the right. Cross another stile over a fence, staying on the broad green track. Bear left to cross a footbridge and stile, then bear right on a path over the grass. Pass through an old hedge-line and soon turn right, to cross a stile in the fence. Head straight across the meadows towards the river. Meet the corner of a field and continue straight on down the hedge and fence. Bear left to cross a stile, within earshot of the weir again. Steps lead up to a footbridge over the river. On the opposite bank a surfaced riverside path leads off to the left. Bear right on this path to return to the car park at the start, passing a slipway for launching small craft.

Walk 6

Studland's Sand and Heath

Easy walking through a significant nature reserve over beach and heath.

•DISTANCE•	7 miles (11.3km)
•MINIMUM TIME•	4hrs
•ASCENT / GRADIENT•	132ft (40m)
•LEVEL OF DIFFICULTY•	
•PATHS•	Sandy beach, muddy heathland tracks, verges, no stiles
•LANDSCAPE•	Sandy Studland Bay, heath and views over Poole Harbour
•SUGGESTED MAP•	aqua3 OS Explorer OL 15 Purbeck & South Dorset
•START / FINISH•	Grid reference: SZ 033835
•DOG FRIENDLINESS•	Not allowed on beach June–September, check locally for precise dates
•PARKING•	Knoll car park, by visitor centre, just off B3351
•PUBLIC TOILETS•	By visitor centre and near ferry toll station

BACKGROUND TO THE WALK

The glorious sands in Studland Bay are justly famous, attracting over one million visitors a year, so you'll need to get up early to have the beach to yourself. You're unlikely to be alone for long and local horseriders are often the first to arrive.

Naked Gape

As you progress up the beach, getting warmer, you can shed your clothes with impunity, for the upper stretch is the less familiar form of nature reserve, opening its arms to naturists. Even on a winter's morning you'll spot brave souls sunbathing naked in the shelter of the marram-covered dunes. Off-shore you'll see big, sleek motor boats – of the 'gin palace' variety – letting rip as they emerge from the constraints of Poole Harbour. Watch out, too, for the orange and blue of the Poole lifeboat on practice manoeuvres, and the yellow and black pilot boat nipping out to lead in the tankers. Jet skiers zip around the more sedate sailing yachts, all dodging the small fishing boats. It's a perfect seaside harmony, complete with 'wheedling' gulls.

Studland's sand is pale gold and fine-ground, trodden by thousands of feet, piled into hundreds of satisfying sand castles and smoothed daily by the sea. The shells underfoot become more numerous as you approach the tip of the sand bar. It's a wonderful opportunity for some shell spotting. Look for the flattish conical mother-of-pearl whorls of topshells, the curious pinky-brown pockets of slipper limpets, the glossy, uneven orange disks of the common saddle oyster and the flat reddish-brown sun-rays of scallops. The deeply ridged fans of common cockles and the vivid blue flash of mussels are a common sight. More challenging is to identify the uneven ellipse of sand gapers or the delicate finger-nail pink of the thin tellin.

Behind the beach lies the rugged heath, part of the same nature reserve, which is in the care of English Nature and the National Trust. These two bodies are currently working together on a programme of restoration. They are reclaiming heath that had become farmland, clearing scrub and maintaining controlled grazing to prevent it all reverting to woodland. I saw my first rare Dartford warbler here, perched on a sprig of gorse – with its pinky brown colouring and long tail, it's a distinctive little bird. All six of Britain's reptiles – common lizard, sand lizard, smooth snake, adder, grass snake and slow-worm – live on the heath. They may be spotted if you know where to look and what you're looking for. Be patient and you might see one soaking up the sunshine in a quiet corner. Trapped between the dunes and the heath is a freshwater lake known as the Little Sea. Hides allow you to watch the dizzying variety of coastal and freshwater birds which congregate here.

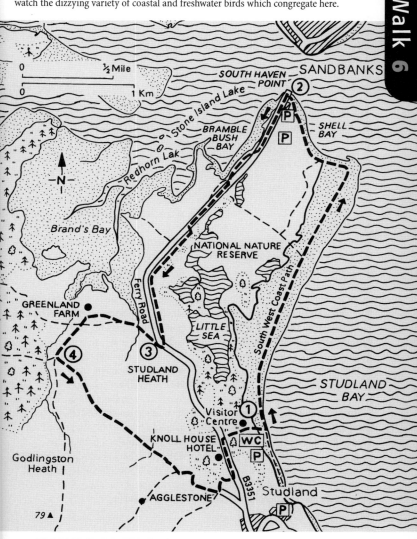

Walk 6 Directions

① From the car park go past the **visitor centre** to the sea. Turn left and walk up the beach for about

2 miles (3.2km). Marram-covered dunes hide the edge of the heath on your left, but you have views to Tennyson Down on the Isle of Wight, and the golden cliffs of Bournemouth curve away ahead.

Continue round the tip of the sand bar into **Shell Bay**. Poole opens out ahead – more precisely, the spit of Sandbanks, with the gleaming white Haven Hotel facing you across the harbour mouth. There are good views of the tree-covered nature reserve island of Brownsea, with Branksea Castle staring boldly out at the eastern end.

> **WHERE TO EAT AND DRINK** ⓘ
>
> The café and restaurant at the **Knoll Visitor Centre** is open all year round, weather permitting. An appetising range of home-made food is on offer, from tea and scones to soup and light lunches. The **Shell Bay Seafood Restaurant** at South Haven Point has great views over Poole Harbour from its terrace.

② Turn inland when you reach **South Haven Point**, joining the road by the phone box. Pass the boatyard and toll booth then bear right at a gate on to a bridleway, leading down to some houseboats. Turn left along the tranquil inner shore of **Poole Harbour** and past **Bramble Bush Bay**. Choose any of the various tracks that lead back up to the road. Cross over and follow the verge until the end of some woods on your left, when you can pick up the broad muddy track on the heath. After ½ mile (800m) this bends left, with views across to the Little Sea. Where the track bends sharply right to meet the road, stay straight ahead on the footpath for a few more paces.

> **WHAT TO LOOK FOR** ⓘ
>
> As you stroll along the beach, look back to the chalky cliffs of the Foreland, with the white arches and stacks of **Old Harry Rocks**. They are the opposite toothy end of the Needles (visible across the channel at the tip of the Isle of Wight), and featured in a classic TV commercial in which a car was lowered on to a grass-covered stack by helicopter.

③ Cross the road by a bus stop and head down the track, indicated by a fingerpost. Go past the marshy end of **Studland Heath** and up to a junction by **Greenland Farm**. Bear left and, just round the next corner, turn left through a gate on to the heath. Go straight along an old hedge-line, pass a barn on the left, and reach a fingerpost.

④ Turn left across the heath (not shown on the fingerpost), aiming for the distant lump of the **Agglestone**. Go through a gate by another fingerpost and continue along the muddy track over the top, passing the Agglestone away to your right. Go down into some woods, turn right over a footbridge and pass through a gate into a lane. Pass several houses then, where blue markers indicate a public bridleway, turn left into a field. Head diagonally right into a green lane and go through a gate at the bottom. Turn left along the verge, pass the Knoll House Hotel and turn right at the signpost to return to the car park.

> **WHILE YOU'RE THERE** ⓘ
>
> A chain **ferry** crosses every few minutes between Sandbanks and South Haven Point, disgorging its 'townies' on to the beach and its cars to hurry off into Portland. From Sandbanks you can catch a ferry, spring and summer, to **Brownsea Island**. Red squirrels are the best-known inhabitants of this 494 acre (200ha) nature reserve, but the lagoon supports an important ternery, and avocets, ruff and other unusual waders are regular visitors. There are many other rare creatures to discover, including 17 species of dragonfly and an endangered species of ant.

The Swanage Eccentric

The peculiar story of a coastal town that not only exported stone but imported it too.

•DISTANCE•	4¼ miles (6.8km)
•MINIMUM TIME•	3hrs
•ASCENT / GRADIENT•	509ft (155m) ▲▲▲
•LEVEL OF DIFFICULTY•	🚶 🚶 🚶
•PATHS•	Grassy paths, rocky tracks, pavements, 4 stiles
•LANDSCAPE•	Spectacular cliff scenery, undulating hills, Swanage town
•SUGGESTED MAP•	aqua3 OS Explorer OL 15 Purbeck & South Dorset
•START / FINISH•	Grid reference: SZ 031773
•DOG FRIENDLINESS•	Some town walking
•PARKING•	Durlston Country Park (charge)
•PUBLIC TOILETS•	Durlston Country Park; behind Heritage Centre on harbour (small charge); Peveril Point

BACKGROUND TO THE WALK

In the early 19th century Swanage was a small, bustling, industrial port that shipped stone from the 60 or so quarries in the area. A growing fashion for seabathing would, in time, change the focus of the town for ever. The real changes to the face of Swanage came, however, with the extraordinary collecting habit of one George Burt, a contractor with an eye for fancy architecture.

Instant Architecture

With his uncle, John Mowlem, a local stonemason and philanthropist, Burt shipped marble from the quarries of Purbeck to London, where old buildings were being knocked down to make way for a new wave of construction. Reluctant to see such splendid stonework discarded, Burt salvaged whole pieces, transported them back in the company ships as ballast, and re-erected them in his home town, giving Swanage an unexpected, instant architectural heritage.

The first influence you see of this man is as you walk past the Town Hall. Burt had donated a reasonably plain and simple building to the town in 1872, but in 1883 he added a façade by Sir Christopher Wren, appropriately in Portland stone, which he had rescued from the front of the Mercers' Hall in London's Cheapside. Architectural commentator Sir Nikolaus Pevsner described its florid carvings of stone fruit and wreaths as 'overwhelmingly undisciplined'. Next, in the park near the pier, are a grand archway removed from Hyde Park Corner, three statues and some columns rescued from Billingsgate Market. There's also an absurd but rather elegant clock tower, removed from the south end of London Bridge in 1867, where it had been set as a memorial to the Duke of Wellington.

Burt's Folly

Durlston Castle is an original folly by Burt dating from 1887, designed from the start as a clifftop restaurant on Durlston Head. It has an unexpected educational element, as useful facts and figures from around the world are carved into great stone slabs set into the walls below – for example, in terms of sunshine, the 'longest day' in London is 16½ hours, while in Spitzbergen it is 3½ months. Burt added a large, segmented stone globe of the world but it's rather grey and a little disappointing.

Railway Revival

George Burt was also influential in bringing the railway to Swanage in 1885 – this gave major impetus to the development of the town as a thriving seaside resort. The railway fell under the Beeching axe in the early 1960s, but was revived by enthusiasts who, early in 2002, at last achieved their ambition of linking back up to the main line station at Wareham. Today the mournful 'poop' of its steam train's whistle can be heard across the Isle of Purbeck as it transports visitors on a nostalgic trip between Swanage and Corfe Castle (▶ Walk 8).

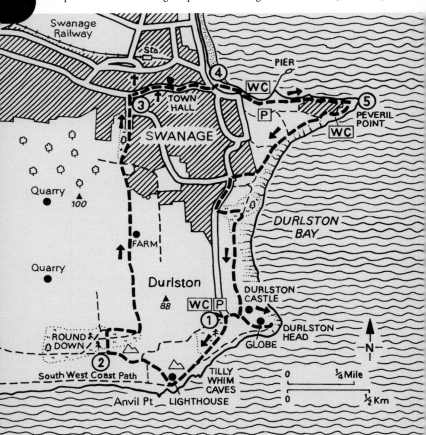

Walk 7 Directions

① Take the footpath directly below the visitor centre car park, signed to the lighthouse. Steps lead down through some trees. With the sea ahead, follow the path round to the right, joining the coastal path. Keep right, towards the lighthouse, down the steep path. As you climb up the other side, look back and down to admire the spectacular **Tilly Whim Caves** cut into the ledges of the cliff. Pass the **lighthouse** and turn right, then go through a kissing gate to follow the path with butterfly markers up the steep side of **Round Down**, with views to St Adhelm's Head (▶ Walk 9).

② At the top bear right, heading inland and parallel with a wall. Go down a slope, through a gate and across a footbridge, then turn up to the right. At a wooden gate turn left over a stone stile, following the butterfly marker. After another stile you can see the roll of the Purbeck Hills ahead and the roofs of Swanage to the right. Cross a stile and go down a broad, grassy track. Beyond a stile by a farm this track narrows and begins to climb steeply. Continue straight ahead on to the road and follow this into the town, with the prominent **church** in front of you.

> ### WHERE TO EAT AND DRINK ⓘ
> You can get a meal at the **Durlston Castle restaurant**, which will also supply you with tea (or something stronger), and ice cream. For my money, however, you can't beat fish and chips eaten down on the harbour, shared with the seagulls and watching the activity in the bay.

③ Turn right on to the main road. It's worth pausing to admire the little square with its butter cross and old stone houses tumbling down to the church. Continue along the street, but look out for: the modest metal plaque above the front door of **No 22A**, home of Taffy Evans; the elaborate **Wesley memorial**; and the extraordinary **Town Hall** with its Wren frontage.

④ At the square bear left beside the **Heritage Centre**, towards the harbour. Turn right and pass the entrance to the pier. Keep left at the

> ### WHILE YOU'RE THERE ⓘ
> Pop into **Studland Heritage Centre** (closed in winter) and learn more about the area, including tales of smuggling and the development of Purbeck's stone quarrying industry. Pay a nominal fee and enjoy the delights of **Swanage's Victorian pier**, which has penny-in-the-slot machines and 'Wot the butler saw' – no seaside visit can be complete without it. The pier suffered in the past from neglect and threat of demolition, but is undergoing restoration.

yellow marker, then bear right, up the hill, past a modern apartment block and a bizarre stone tower, to reach the tip of **Peveril Point**, with its coastguard station.

⑤ Turn right and walk up the grassy slope along the top of the cliffs. Take the path in the top corner and follow the Victoria's head markers to a road. Turn left through an area of pleasant Victorian villas. Erosion of the coastal path means a well-signed detour here, along the street, down to the left and left into woodland, signposted to the lighthouse. Follow the path for about ½ mile (800m) along the cliff top to **Durlston Head**. Pass **Durlston Castle** on your left and turn down to examine Burt's great stone globe. Stagger back up the steep hill to return to the car park.

> ### WHAT TO LOOK FOR ⓘ
> On the High Street, the small terraced house at **No 22A** bears a modest metal plaque above the front door, announcing that this was the home of Petty Officer Edgar 'Taffy' Evans. An experienced seaman, he was described by a companion as 'a giant worker'. He perished with Captain Scott from the effects of frostbite and exhaustion on the way back from the South Pole in 1912.

Worth Matravers to Corfe

Journey between a docile quarry village and a condemned castle.

•DISTANCE•	9 miles (14.5km)
•MINIMUM TIME•	3hrs
•ASCENT / GRADIENT•	1,083ft (330m) ▲▲▲
•LEVEL OF DIFFICULTY•	🚶 🚶 🚶
•PATHS•	Village lanes, rocky lanes (slippery after rain), moorland tracks, grassy paths, steep cliff path with steps, 34 stiles
•LANDSCAPE•	Fields and tracks, path, coastal path
•SUGGESTED MAP•	aqua3 OS Explorer OL 15 Purbeck & South Dorset
•START / FINISH•	Grid reference: SY 974776
•DOG FRIENDLINESS•	Good, though some stiles challenging
•PARKING•	Car park just north of Worth Matravers (honesty box)
•PUBLIC TOILETS•	At car park; also Corfe Castle by car park

BACKGROUND TO THE WALK

Worth Matravers is a picturesque village of lichen-encrusted grey cottages, complete with duck pond. But for its windswept position, huddled in a cleft above the coast, it is reminiscent of many a Cotswold beauty spot. Men from here have worked the nearby quarries for centuries and local stone was used to build Salisbury Cathedral.

By contrast, the huge and toothy ruin of Corfe Castle seems to fill the gap in the wall of the Purbeck Hills with its presence. It stands on a high mound, and must have been massively imposing when whole. The castle has a grim history. In AD 978 a youthful King Edward (the Martyr) was murdered here while visiting his stepmother, Elfthryth. His body was buried without ceremony at Wareham, while his half-brother took the throne as Ethelred II. However, stories of miracles occurring soon resulted in Edward's body being exhumed and transported to Shaftesbury, where an abbey grew up in his honour. His sacred relics were recovered in 1931 and reburied, incredibly, not in an abbey but in Brookwood Cemetery, to the west of London. Elfthryth, consumed with guilt, retreated to a nunnery.

The Normans realised the commanding role a castle could play in defence at Corfe. In around 1106, the big square keep was built. King John starved 22 French noblemen to death in the dungeons here in 1204 and used it as a lifelong prison for his niece Eleanor, a potential threat to his throne. The unfortunate Edward II, deposed by his wife Isabella and her favourite, Roger de Mortimer, was also imprisoned here briefly.

The castle again came to the fore during the Civil War. Its owner, Sir John Bankes, having sought and failed to make peace between factions, sided with the King. However, it was his spirited wife Mary who was left, with a handful of women and just five men, to fight off a siege in 1642, when a 500-strong Parliamentarian army reached Corfe Castle. It is said that the Roundheads took the lead from the church roof to make their bullets and stored their powder and shot in the organ pipes. Despite reinforcements, they failed to take the castle. After a second, more sustained siege, the castle was betrayed in 1646 by one of its defenders and Lady Bankes was forced to give it up. The castle was deliberately destroyed, to prevent its further use. Close up, the sagging towers of the gatehouse and the crazy angle of the outer walls give the impression that they were blown up only days ago.

Walk 8

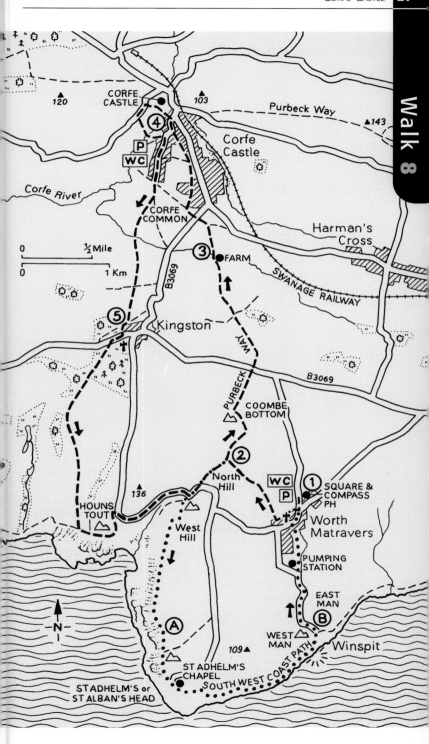

Walk 8

Walk 8 Directions

① Turn right down the street and soon go right, up a path by a fingerpost. Cross a stile and turn left through a gap in the wall, walking behind the village. Turn right at the end, cross the wall and continue down the next field. At the bottom bear left over the stile, walking down a narrow cutting.

② Cross two stiles and turn right on to the **Purbeck Way** (left if only following Walk 9). Follow the track up the valley, bending left at **Coombe Bottom** and right through a gate and up a hill. Go through the gate at the top, then bear right on to a track. At the farm turn left then right to meet the road. Cross and turn left down the track, signed 'Purbeck Way'. Stay on this to the bottom of the hill. By some fir trees turn left, cross a footbridge and turn right. Pass a farm and go straight down on to the heath.

③ After a footbridge, go straight on over **Corfe Common** towards the castle. Bear left at a marker, and right to a gate. Cross the **B3069**, go through a gate and straight on, later bearing right behind houses. Go through a gate and follow the path towards the village centre. After it narrows turn right, through a gate, and go across fields into a playground. Turn left then right into **West Street** to the square.

> **WHAT TO LOOK FOR** ⓘ
> On the far side of **St Nicholas' Church** in Worth Matravers are buried members of the Jesty family. Enlightened dairy farmer Benjamin Jesty was the first person to experiment (on his own wife and sons, in 1774) with cow pox as an inoculation against smallpox.

④ Turn left by the **castle** on the path below the walls. Go left up the road and soon left again by a gate and over a stile. Cross the fields to a car park. Here bear left then right on to **West Street**. At the end, go straight on over a cattle grid. Bear left on a path across the heath. Cross duckboards and go uphill, bearing right between a stone block and a tumulus. Go down the other side and through a gate. Cross two bridges and go up through a gap between trees, then ahead across a field and into a green droving lane. Cross another field, go straight over a road and up the hill. Walk up the next field, heading towards Kingston church tower.

> **WHERE TO EAT AND DRINK** ⓘ
> In the **Square and Compasses** in Worth Matravers they serve pasties with a range of real ales. The **Worth Matravers Teashop** serves Dorset honey cream teas. In Corfe Castle, the **Fox Inn** offers pies, fillet steak and baguettes. Dogs and smokers are welcome inside but children are confined to the garden.

⑤ At the top, go through a gate, and turn right. Immediately after a junction of lanes, turn left, up through some trees, then bear left to a road. Turn right, soon taking the track on the left, signposted 'Houns Tout'. Follow this to the sea and along the exposed cliff tops. Descend steps, then cross a stile at the bottom. Head inland to a road. Turn right and follow it round, bearing left on to a track signed 'Coastal Path'. Beside a house bear right, downhill. Go through a gate and continue straight ahead up the road (or join Walk 9). Where this swings right, keep straight on up to **Beacon Bottom**. After ¼ mile (400m) turn right over the stile and retrace your steps to the car park.

Coast Path to St Adhelm's

A shorter clifftop circuit around dramatic St Adhelms's Head.
See map and information panel for Walk 8

•DISTANCE•	5 miles (8km)
•MINIMUM TIME•	2hrs
•ASCENT / GRADIENT•	919ft (280m) ▲▲ ▲
•LEVEL OF DIFFICULTY•	👣 👣 👣

Walk 9 Directions
(Walk 8 option)

Leave Walk 8 at Point ② by turning left on to the **Purbeck Way**. Go straight downhill and join a road. Bear left through a gate into a field, and immediately fork left, steeply uphill. Bear right along the wall at the brow and follow the path along the top of the cliffs. Pass a garden **memorial** to Royal Marines killed between 1945 and 1990 on the left. Cross a stile and continue down the path, Point Ⓐ.

Follow the path as it descends into the steep ravine via turf steps. Head up the other side – there are 204 steps! Pass a row of coastguard cottages and **St Adhelm's Chapel**, which is up a short track. A sturdy, buttressed, brown cube with just one tiny window, the chapel is 800 years old. Return to the coast path by the **coastguard station**, passing a gleaming steel memorial to the work of radar developers in the 1940s, set above the remains of the wartime station.

The old coastguard station at St Adhelm's has been restored by the National Coastwatch Institution, an organisation which maintains a visual and radio distress watch out to sea as a support to HM Coastguard. The NCI stations are manned by unpaid, trained volunteers, many of whom are ex-fishermen.

Continue on the coastal path, down towards Winspit, with good views to Durlston lighthouse. The big dark patch in the cliffs immediately ahead is the huge cave by Dancing Ledge. The footpath curls up to the left above the abandoned quarry and buildings of **Winspit**, Point Ⓑ.

Descend some steps and turn left. The lane leads inland up a leafy valley, and it's suddenly very quiet away from the sea. Pass **Winspit Cottage** on the right and continue on the track, climbing gently, between hills called **East Man** and **West Man**. The houses of the village come into view and there is evidence of strip lynchets (like big terraces) up on the hillside on the right. Where the track forks by a **pumping station**, turn right on to a grassy path, then cross a stile and bear left up the field. Cross a stile at the far side, go up a rocky path, then straight ahead, into the village. Turn left up through the little garden to reach the pond. Turn right up the main road, passing the pub, to return to the car park.

The Blue Pool Beauty Spot

Circling the unlikely by-product of an industrial process.

•DISTANCE•	3½ miles (5.7km)
•MINIMUM TIME•	1hr 30min
•ASCENT / GRADIENT•	165ft (50m)
•LEVEL OF DIFFICULTY•	
•PATHS•	Country lanes, heath and woodland tracks (may be boggy)
•LANDSCAPE•	Heath, woodland, rolling country
•SUGGESTED MAP•	aqua3 OS Explorer OL 15 Purbeck & South Dorset
•START / FINISH•	Grid reference: SY 931837
•DOG FRIENDLINESS•	Some roadwalking
•PARKING•	At roadside just south of phone box in Furzebrook
•PUBLIC TOILETS•	None on route, unless visiting Blue Pool

Walk 10 Directions

Walk south on the main road through the village, passing the drive to **Furzebrook House** on the left. Furzebrook is an unremarkable estate village of Victorian houses and its roads are stained white by the lorries from the claypits. Furzebrook House is once more a private house. Commandeered during the Second World War, it was in such poor shape by the end of it that the Barnards refused to take it back – it became, instead, a government research establishment, which it remained for many years. At the end of the park wall turn left

WHILE YOU'RE THERE

On the western edge of the village of Church Knowle is a different sort of retirement centre – it's the extensive **Margaret Green Foundation Trust Animal Sanctuary**, where domestic, farm and wild animals come to retire, or to find a new home. There's even an aviary for lost, injured or oiled birds. Admission is by donation and there's a gift shop to help support the sanctuary's work.

down a straight drive, signed to the Blue Pool. Descend gently, to pass a parking area on the left and then the entrance to the **Blue Pool** on the right.

The Blue Pool is a real beauty spot on the Furzebrook Estate. It was first opened to the public by T T Barnard in 1935 and is owned by his daughter today. Gloriously set amid trees, the pool itself is an old clay pit filled with rainwater. Minute clay particles, that are suspended in the water, refract the sunlight, giving the pool its extraordinary, deep turquoise colour. The body of water refracts colours differently according to light and temperature conditions and is seen at its most vivid blue on a cold, grey day, when the clay particles rise more towards the surface of the lake. At other times it may appear emerald green. There are lots of woodland paths to explore, as well as an adventure playground for children. You can enjoy the beautiful setting on this walk, whether or not the pool itself is open (March to November).

Walk 10

Continue straight ahead, up the track into the woods, and soon emerge at the edge of an area of heath, dotted with Scots pines. Stay on the main track (ignore a path to the left), go through a kissing gate and follow the yellow marker on to the heath. Shortly after this, look for a post on your left, indicating that the footpath leaves the vehicular track. Bear left on the peaty path through gorse and heather, following green **Purbeck Heritage** markers. Go through another kissing gate. Turn right up the track at the marker stone, signed 'East Creech'.

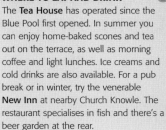

WHERE TO EAT AND DRINK

The **Tea House** has operated since the Blue Pool first opened. In summer you can enjoy home-baked scones and tea out on the terrace, as well as morning coffee and light lunches. Ice creams and cold drinks are also available. For a pub break or in winter, try the venerable **New Inn** at nearby Church Knowle. The restaurant specialises in fish and there's a beer garden at the rear.

WHAT TO LOOK FOR

Clay was dug here in the 17th century for use in the manufacture of clay pipes and later as a component of china manufacturing in the potteries of Staffordshire, most notably at Wedgwood. This story is told in the little museum by the Blue Pool and occasionally a pipe-maker is on hand to demonstrate.

Continue past a forest of drunken birch trees on your left, then through pretty woodland dripping with moss and lichen. Cross a sleeper bridge over a marsh, where the water is stained orange by iron ore. Pass through some pines, with a pool on the left, and continue along the boundary fence – you'll hear a waterfall off to the left.

At a junction of paths (with bridges to your left) go straight on, following the blue marker, again signposted 'East Creech'. Pass a reedy pool on the left. Keep straight ahead on the broad track (part of the Purbeck Way) that leads up through the woods. Pass a larger pool up on the right – it looks the sort of place where Henry Thoreau would have built his cabin. The soil

underfoot is black and springy with peat. Look for the old holly trees with ferns growing all over them.

At the road turn left and walk down to a junction. Turn right here and walk up the road into **East Creech** village. This is an attractive corner of farmland and little hills. Pass **Creech Farm** with its duck pond, and a pretty pair of cottages: **Wild Rose** and **Rockley**. Keep right past the post box and walk along the valley, with distant views to Poole and Bournemouth. Pass some woods on the left and the high point of **Creech Barrow Hill**, also to your left. The road rises steadily to pass a big thatched house, again on the left. As the road starts to descend there are magnificent views inland over the Isle of Purbeck, with Wareham ahead. Turn right along a lane just before a farm and soon cross a stile to the right (before the farm gate). Turn left then bear right, down the field to the corner. Cross over the stile and bear diagonally left down the hill, following yellow markers across the heath, through trees and gorse. Go through an area of beeches, with bracken below. Pass between a shed and a garden fence, then pass a house on the right and walk straight ahead to meet the road. Turn left and retrace your steps through **Furzebrook** to the start.

The Royal Forest of Cranborne

Exploring extensive plantations on the steeply rolling landscape of a Norman royal hunting forest.

•DISTANCE•	4 miles (6.4km)
•MINIMUM TIME•	2hrs
•ASCENT / GRADIENT•	165ft (50m) ▲▲▲
•LEVEL OF DIFFICULTY•	🚶 🚶 🚶
•PATHS•	Woodland paths and tracks, quiet roads, farm paths, 3 stiles
•LANDSCAPE•	Woods and valleys of Cranborne Chase
•SUGGESTED MAP•	aqua3 OS Explorer 118 Shaftesbury & Cranborne Chase
•START / FINISH•	Grid reference: SU 003194
•DOG FRIENDLINESS•	Strict control required in RSPB woods; one unfriendly stile
•PARKING•	Garston Wood car park (free), on Bowerchalke road 2 miles (3.2km) north of Sixpenny Handley
•PUBLIC TOILETS•	None on route

BACKGROUND TO THE WALK

Cranborne Chase covers around 100 square miles (259sq km) of the long chalk massif which straddles the Dorset/Wiltshire border east of Shaftesbury. Once a royal hunting preserve, it is now mostly rolling grassland with pockets of mixed woodland. Compared with other parts of Dorset, there are few settlements here, a sign of the feudal state in which the land was held until 1830. Like most of southern England after the last Ice Age, Dorset became smothered in a natural growth of native, broadleaved woodland, such as oak, ash and elm. As the human population grew and spread, this woodland was gradually cleared, firstly for its valuable timber and secondly to make way for agricultural land. The hunting 'forest' of Cranborne Chase claimed by William the Conqueror therefore included open sections of heath, downland, scrub and rough pasture, as well as patches of remaining woodland. Little original forest remains on the Chase – most woods show signs of mixed planting and of many generations of coppicing.

Industrial Trees

The effects of planting for timber in the late 18th century can be seen in the widespread stands of non-native beech across the Chase. Trees for timber were planted compactly to encourage tall, straight growth with a minimum of interruption from side branches.

Coppicing, the chief form of woodland management, was designed to produce a continuous supply of timber for everyday use. Hazel that was cut back or coppiced when young would grow long, straight poles. Repeating the exercise produced a steady supply of timber for thatching spars, hurdles and other uses. The resulting multi-stemmed growths, or stools, can be seen today all over Dorset's woods and include oak, ash, alder, sweet chestnut and even sycamore. In Garston Wood you can see the effects of modern coppicing in action on hazel and field maple. The seven to eight year cycle of cutting means that there are different stages of tree development within the one wood, creating more light and space than if it were left unmanaged. This produces an optimum habitat for wildlife, including sunlight-loving butterflies such as the silver washed fritillary and purple hairstreak.

Deerhunters, Poachers and Smugglers

The pursuit of fallow deer on the Chase provided the mainstay of royal sport. The deer can still be seen here, especially in the early evening. Cranborne Chase changed hands many times. The hunting rights were acquired by King John and retained by most succeeding monarchs until the 17th century. In 1714 they passed to the Pitt-Rivers family, who ruled the area like feudal overlords. Operating under so-called Chase Law and free from the constraints of normal policing, Cranborne became a byway for smugglers and a refuge for criminals, often with bloody results – especially when conflicts arose over poaching. In 1830, after considerable local pressure, Chase Law was abandoned and consequently life became a little more settled.

Walk 11

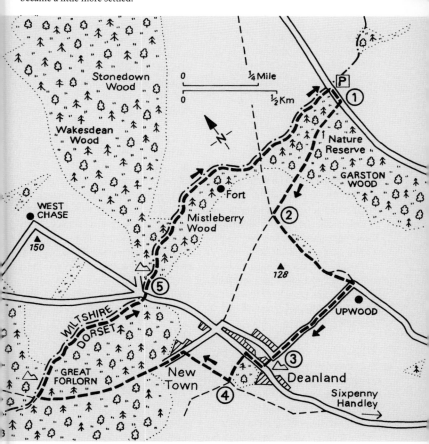

Walk 11 Directions

① Go through the gate in the corner and take the broad track that

leads up through the woods. Go straight ahead through a kissing gate and emerge at the corner of a field. Keep right, up the edge of this field, and continue straight on.

Walk 11

② At a junction of tracks turn left and walk alongside the hedge, on a waymarked bridleway, through rolling farmland dotted with trees. The muddy farm track leads gently downhill. Where it sweeps left into the farm, go straight ahead on a grassy track. Pass some cow byres on the left, with **Upwood farmhouse** largely hidden in some trees ahead, and turn right along the lane. Continue through a gate, along an old avenue of sycamores between high banks and hedges.

> **WHILE YOU'RE THERE** ℹ
> **Sixpenny Handley** has one of the oddest names in England, which alone justifies a visit. The prefix derives from a mix of English and Celtic words and means 'hill of the Saxons'. Much of the old village was destroyed in a fire of 1892. Today it's a bold, lively and modern village with lots of new housing.

③ Pass a house on the right and bear left on a steep, narrow path straight down the hill to emerge on a road, in the hamlet of **Deanland**. Turn right, pass a phone box and reach a gate on the left, with a yellow marker. Go through, bear diagonally right across a small field to cross a stile, then bear left up the edge of the field, with woods to your left.

④ Look for a stile on your left, but turn directly right here, to walk across the field, parallel with the road. Over the brow of the hill ahead, the pleasing higgledy-piggledy settlement of **New Town** can be seen. Head for the stile in the bottom corner of the field. Turn left up the lane, which becomes a broad, woodland track. Follow this for ½ mile (800m). By the entrance to a conifer wood, eloquently named the **Great Forlorn**, look for

> **WHERE TO EAT AND DRINK** ℹ
> The **Roebuck Inn** free house at Sixpenny Handley serves real ale and traditional, home-cooked food in its bright and airy front restaurant. Try lasagne, cod and chips, baguettes, jacket potatoes or tackle the poached salmon on the fuller menu. A roast Sunday lunch is served throughout the winter. In summer you can enjoy the large beer garden. Dogs are welcome in the garden, supervised children are allowed in the restaurant.

the yellow marker and turn right up the hill. After a steep climb it levels out, with fields on your left. Keep straight on, with good views across to West Chase house, at the head of its own valley. Descend steadily, then cross a stile to emerge at a road by a **lodge house**.

⑤ Cross straight over on to a broad track and immediately turn up to the right on a narrow path beside a fence. Follow this straight up the hill through the woods – it levels out towards the top, with fields on the left. At a junction of tracks keep left then bear right, continuing along the edge of the wood, and eventually descending to reach the road. Turn right to return to the car park at Garston Wood.

> **WHAT TO LOOK FOR** ℹ
> Listen for the **nightingale**'s song in Garston Wood. The RSPB is trying to balance its needs against those of the endangered turtle dove in its management of the wood. In the early 1980s a young commercial plantation of beech, larch and Corsican pine drew the nightingales. By 1993 the dense understorey in which they thrived had been smothered by the tree canopy, and they disappeared. The plantation is gradually being felled and replanted to provide a suitable habitat to woo the nightingales back.

Roads and Residents at Badbury Rings

An easy, longish walk on the edge of the Kingston Lacey Estate.

•DISTANCE•	7½ miles (12.1km)
•MINIMUM TIME•	4hrs
•ASCENT / GRADIENT•	459ft (140m) ▲ ▲▲ ▲▲
•LEVEL OF DIFFICULTY•	炸炸 炸炸 炸炸
•PATHS•	Farm tracks, roads, grassy lanes and fields, 15 stiles
•LANDSCAPE•	Gently rolling farmland leading down to water-meadows
•SUGGESTED MAP•	aqua3 OS Explorer 118 Shaftesbury & Cranborne Chase
•START / FINISH•	Grid reference: ST 959031
•DOG FRIENDLINESS•	Not allowed on Badbury Rings site; some roadwalking
•PARKING•	Car park (donation) at Badbury Rings, signposted off B3082 from Wimborne to Blandford
•PUBLIC TOILETS•	None on route

BACKGROUND TO THE WALK

The most obvious and lasting legacy of the Roman invasion of Britain in AD 43 is the network of straight military roads that they constructed, like a spider's web, across the country. Before they came, many of the routes may have already existed as tracks, but it took the Roman desire for effective communication and control across their empire to make these permanent – there are many stretches still in use today. A few roads would have actually been paved, but usually fine gravel was layered over coarser chippings for effective drainage (a forerunner of modern tarmac).

Roman Interchange

Four of the most important Roman routes across Dorset met at the hub of Badbury Rings. The most famous and visible of these is Ackling Dyke, the major road which linked London (Londinium) with Old Sarum (Sorviodunum), Dorchester (Durnovaria, the civitas or Roman capital of the Dorset area) and Exeter (Iscarduniorum).

Badbury Rings was a massive fort, occupying a spectacular vantage point. Bronze-Age burial barrows in the area confirm a settlement here around 2000 BC, and the rings and ditches of the fort date from the 6th century BC. At that time Dorset was inhabited by the Durotriges tribe, who were prosperous Iron-Age traders, farmers and potters.

The indications are that the Second Augusta Legion, under the command of Vespasian (who would later become Emperor) had built an advance base at Lake Farm, beside the River Stour at Wimborne. They realised the strategic importance of Badbury and, at some time in the early years of the invasion, the Legionaries attacked and took control of the hill top. The fort was systematically dismantled, the unlucky inhabitants killed, sold into slavery or otherwise dispersed.

The Romans went on to build their own fortified citadel called Vindocladia, near by at Shapwick. When the Romans finally withdrew from Britain in the 5th century, this site was absorbed back into the Dorset landscape, like so many other Roman structures.

Badbury Rings did not disappear from history however. Many believe that it was the site of Mount Badon, or Mons Badonicus, where King Arthur fought and won a legendary battle against the Saxons around AD 516. In 1645 the fort served as a meeting place for the Dorset Clubmen, a ragged, badly armed force opposing both parties in the Civil War. Over 4,000 gathered to hear speeches by local notables. The meeting alerted Cromwell to their threat and they were subsequently routed by his New Model Army (▶ Walk 23).

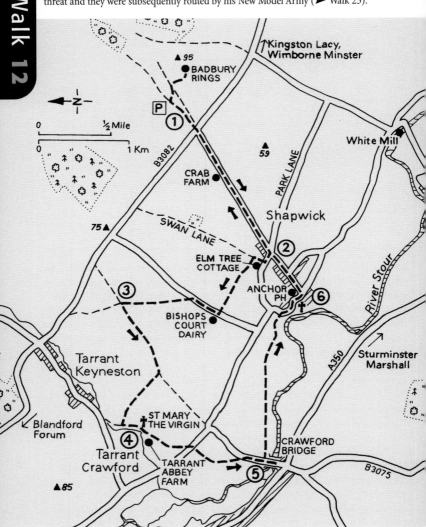

Walk 12 Directions

① Walk up the hill to explore **Badbury Rings**, then head down the track by which you drove in.

Cross the **B3082** and go straight down the road towards Shapwick – its straightness gives away its Roman origins. Pass **Crab Farm**, with Charborough Tower on the distant horizon.

Walk 12

② At the junction with **Park Lane** turn right, then right again by **Elm Tree Cottage** to go up **Swan Lane**, a grassy track. Turn left over a stile before the gate. Go straight over the field, cross a stile, and along the edge of the next field. Cross the stile into the yard of **Bishops Court Dairy** and turn right past the first barn. At the gates bear left over a stile, then right across the field, heading for a stile half-way along the hedge. Cross this and bear right to the top corner of the field.

WHERE TO EAT AND DRINK ⓘ

The red brick **Anchor** free house in the centre of Shapwick village goes out of its way to welcome families (and dogs are welcome at the bar end). Aside from staples such as home-made steak and mushroom pie, for something more exotic, try the kangaroo braised in port. There's also a good vegetarian choice.

---

③ Cross a stile and turn left down the broad bridleway. After about ½ mile (800m) pass a line of trees. Turn right, up a track between high hedges (following the blue public bridleway marker). Continue walking downhill, with glimpses of Tarrant Crawford church blending into trees on your left. Follow the track round to the left, by the side of a stream.

④ Go through a gate and reach the **church** on your left. Continue towards the barns of **Tarrant Abbey Farm**. Now go left through a gate and continue diagonally across the field to a track between fences. Follow this uphill, passing above the farmhouse. At the top of the track cross a stile and go straight over the next field. Cross the road and walk down the edge of the field. Cross another road into a green lane. Bear left across a stile and then

---

WHAT TO LOOK FOR ⓘ

Don't miss the little grey **Abbey Church of St Mary the Virgin** in Tarrant Crawford. Once a nunnery, its simple interior has dark box pews, panelling around the altar and a Jacobean pulpit. Some details of its 14th-century wall-painting of the legend of St Margaret of Antioch are still discernible. A brass cross in the floor commemorates where rector Francis Alfred Smith dropped dead after giving evensong in July 1877, at the tender age of 35.

---

diagonally across a field. Go through a gate on to the road and turn right.

⑤ Walk on to the old **Crawford Bridge**, just to admire it. Retrace your steps and turn right at the footpath sign. Cross a stile and walk straight across the meadows for a mile (1.6km). When you reach a fence on the left, walk around it to a gate. Go through and follow the track round to the right. Cross a stile behind the farm and walk along the road into the village.

⑥ Pass the **Anchor** pub and turn left, passing **Piccadilly Lane** on your right-hand side. Go straight up the road, now retracing your route back to the car park at **Badbury Rings**.

WHILE YOU'RE THERE ⓘ

In an idyllic setting beside the River Stour at Sturminster Marshall is **White Mill**, a beautifully restored corn mill. Just to the west of Wimborne you'll find **Kingston Lacy**, a delightful mansion set in vast parkland. Built in 1663 for the Bankes family after the destruction of their previous home in Corfe Castle (▶ Walk 8), today the house has a particularly fine collection of paintings. Both the mill and the house are preserved by the National Trust.

Tarrant Gunville and Pimperne Long Barrow

A stroll across open farmland in search of an ancient tomb.

•DISTANCE•	5 miles (8km)
•MINIMUM TIME•	2hrs
•ASCENT / GRADIENT•	360ft (110m) ▲ ▲ ▲
•LEVEL OF DIFFICULTY•	🕺 🕺 🕺
•PATHS•	Quiet country lanes, farm and woodland tracks, no stiles
•LANDSCAPE•	Rolling farmland with clumps of deciduous woodland
•SUGGESTED MAP•	aqua3 OS Explorer 118 Shaftesbury & Cranborne Chase
•START / FINISH•	Grid reference: ST 925128
•DOG FRIENDLINESS•	Some roadwalking
•PARKING•	Up broad lane beside village hall in Tarrant Gunville
•PUBLIC TOILETS•	None on route

BACKGROUND TO THE WALK

The chalk downs of Dorset are littered with burial mounds of our ancestors. The long barrow on the hill above Pimperne is one of several in the immediate area and marks the site of a neolithic settlement dating from around 3000 BC. A contemporary earthwork is shown on the map, but it has been ploughed into the ground. Down the slope towards the road is a later round barrow, or tumulus. A similar settlement site and earthwork is marked above the Ninety Nine Plantation on a neighbouring slope to the north east (► Walk 14); there are more tumuli here, also disappearing under the plough, and a less impressively preserved long barrow. The settlers in this part of England are believed to have come over from the Continent. They were farmers, introducing cattle and sheep to Britain from south eastern Europe and the Middle East.

Communal Graves

Pimperne's long barrow is one of the best in Dorset. It appears as a 330ft long (101m), scrub-covered mound at the edge of a field. Long barrows like this were communal graves, usually for men with the status of chiefs and for their families. The barrows consisted of mounded earth and stone. There were commonly six to eight bodies inside, sometimes buried with vessels of food and possibly interred over a long period of time.

Often, as with the example of the Grey Mare and her Colts (► Walk 38), the long barrows would be divided into small chambers by large, flat slabs of stone. With the surrounding fields full of tiny flints, it is easy to see that such luxuries were not available here, and so timber was probably used instead. However, the flinty ground was important to the neolithic settlers for other reasons. A legacy of finely-worked spear heads, arrow heads and polished stone axes shows the value of this hard stone in their daily lives, both for immediate use and for trading. (There's a good collection in the museum in Dorchester.)

Burial mounds of different sorts are found all over Dorset. The round barrows are probably the most common. They date from around 2000 BC and were usually single graves. Other later forms include the bell barrow, where the mound was surrounded by a ditch, and the bowl barrow, where the body was buried in a crouching position. So-called disc barrows, clearly visible in aerial photographs of nearby Oakley Down, consist of one or two small mounds on a larger circle of flat ground, surrounded by a ditch and bank. Finds of beads and needles amid the cremated remains suggest these may have been the burial place of high-born women. The construction of barrows continued under the Roman occupation, only ceasing around AD 750.

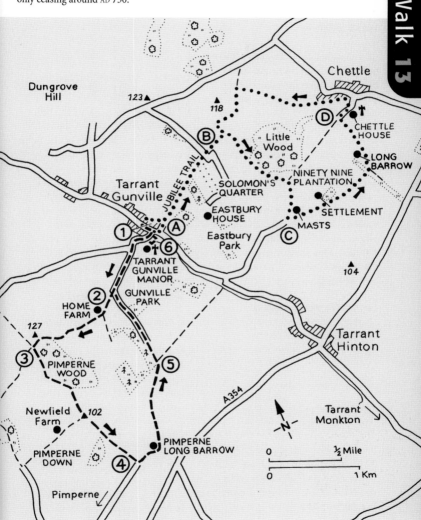

Walk 13 Directions

① Turn left on the main street, passing the phone box on your right. Turn right by the old forge,

signposted 'Everley Hill', and go up the road. Where it swings right, keep straight ahead up the lane. Pass the gates of the **Manor House**, on the left. At a junction keep straight ahead on the farm track.

② Pass an old farmhouse on the right, with a pocket-sized labourer's cottage in the yard. At the fingerpost bear right on the track, passing a fine, old hedge on the right. The route climbs gently uphill, passing the end of **Pimperne Wood** on the left.

③ At a junction of tracks at the top turn second-left on to the muddy bridleway along the edge of the wood. At the end of the wood stay on the grass track. Where a farm road bends right follow the blue markers straight ahead up the edge of the fields. As you go over the crest of the hill, the bristling radio mast of Blandford army camp is prominent in the view ahead of you. Beyond rolling **Pimperne Down** to the right you can see where Hambledon Hill (➤ Walk 23) falls away sharply to the north. Continue to where the track meets a metalled farm road.

> **WHERE TO EAT AND DRINK** ℹ
> Beside the church, in the impossibly pretty village of Tarrant Monkton, is the red brick **Langton Arms**. Dogs and children are welcome in the public bar and there's also a family room. Good food is served to a steady stream of customers all day on Saturdays and Sundays and at more restricted hours during the week.

④ Turn left on to the grassy track, passing the shell of a barn and a water tower. Go through the gate to **Pimperne Long Barrow**. Walk around the southern end and up the other side, heading diagonally right over the field. Cross a broken-down fence and aim for the grassy track (signified by the blue marker of a public bridleway). Follow this through a field, with woods on your left-hand side.

> **WHAT TO LOOK FOR** ℹ
> A simple **marble plaque** at St Mary's Church in Tarrant Gunville commemorates Thomas Wedgwood, third son of Josiah the Staffordshire potter. He died at Eastbury in 1805, aged 34. Thomas's early experiments in photography brought him a small claim to fame – he worked out how to create images, but unfortunately not how to fix them. His elder brother, another Josiah, occupied nearby Gunville Manor.

⑤ Just over the brow of the hill, where the track veers to the right, bear left down the edge of the field, passing into the woods at the bottom and continuing up the opposite slope. At the top of the hill, by a metal gate, go straight ahead down the green path, which becomes a lane – you'll pass dwellings on the right and skirt the edge of **Gunville Park**. At a junction of lanes turn right and retrace your steps towards the village of **Tarrant Gunville**.

⑥ Bear right before the bottom of the hill through two gates into the churchyard. Leave the church and go down the path and some steps, turning left at the bottom. Turn right at the end, to retrace your steps back into the village.

> **WHILE YOU'RE THERE** ℹ
> **Larmer Tree Gardens** at Tollard Royal were planted with an educational purpose by the famous 19th-century archaeologist Augustus Pitt-Rivers. The larmer tree was an old wych elm, a meeting point for King John and his huntsmen, that blew down in 1894. There's a water garden complete with Roman temple and buildings imported from Nepal. Jazz and brass bands occasionally play in the open-air theatre. The gardens are open throughout the summer, but not on Saturdays.

In Fine Fettle at Chettle

A second walk through the Tarrant Valley's ancient landscape.
See map and information panel for Walk 13

•DISTANCE•	5½ miles (8.8km)
•MINIMUM TIME•	3hrs
•ASCENT / GRADIENT•	360ft (110m) ▲▲ ▲▲ ▲
•LEVEL OF DIFFICULTY•	🚶 🚶 🚶

Walk 14 Directions (Walk 13 option)

Walk through the village and turn left up **School Lane** (Point Ⓐ). Pass the old school, turn left between the houses and continue right to a gate. Follow **Jubilee Trail** markers and bear left up through the woods. Go through a gate into the park of **Eastbury House**.

Go straight up the hill beside the avenue of beeches. At the top cross a stile, left, and follow the lane up to your right. Through a gap in the hedge to your right note the curious parallel lines of regular grassy hummocks in **Solomon's Quarter**, Point Ⓑ. Go straight over a metalled road and cross a stile into a field. At the top of the field bear left and soon go right, over a stile. Turn right, down the edge of the field, signed 'Jubilee Way'. The path runs through woodland. Where it sweeps sharply left, turn right and pass a gate on to a grassy track. This leads along an overgrown ditch and bank, probably the remains of an ancient settlement to your left.

Pass two telecommunications masts and turn left (Point Ⓒ), walking back diagonally down across the field. Cross a farm track and a stile to pass below a large clump of trees (**Ninety Nine Plantation**). Go straight across the next field, aiming for a break in the trees and a yellow marker on the fence. Cross a pair of stiles and go through the narrow belt of woodland. Turn left up the bridleway for a few paces, then walk diagonally right across the field to a gap in the hedge (blue marker). Go straight through, pass the end of a long barrow, and down between a fence and a line of trees. The path becomes a track, dipping down and up through a gateway. Look right for a glimpse of the back of Chettle House, a modest Queen Anne affair.

Emerge at a lane (Point Ⓓ), turn right and head down towards the church. Take the footpath opposite into a farmyard. Follow the yellow marker left up a short track into a field, passing along the back of the village. At the far corner of the field go through the gate and up the hill to meet a bridleway at the top. Turn left. Bear right just after the hedge. Walk round the field edge and turn right at the stile. Retrace your route into **Tarrant Gunville**. Just after the old school take the path on the right, past a recreation ground. Turn left at the end, and at the main road turn left and left again to return to the start.

The Cursus of Gussage St Michael

An easy walk with sweeping views over the remains of an ancient earthwork.

•DISTANCE•	5¼ miles (8.4km)
•MINIMUM TIME•	3hrs
•ASCENT / GRADIENT•	246ft (75m) ▲▲▲
•LEVEL OF DIFFICULTY•	🚶 🚶 🚶
•PATHS•	Firm tracks and green lanes (muddy after rain), 5 stiles
•LANDSCAPE•	Arable farmland and pasture dotted with ancient remains
•SUGGESTED MAP•	aqua3 OS Explorer 118 Shaftesbury & Cranborne Chase
•START / FINISH•	Grid reference: ST 986115
•DOG FRIENDLINESS•	Leads required through farmyards; some roadwalking
•PARKING•	Lay-by in lane opposite garage, by entrance to Lower Farm, Gussage St Michael
•PUBLIC TOILETS•	None on route

Walk 15 Directions

Turn left down the street in Gussage St Michael. It's a small, sprawling village, squeezed between the Roman road of **Ackling Dyke** and a more ancient, processional way known as the **Dorset Cursus**. After passing a repair garage on your right, turn right by **Corner Cottage**, on to the road signposted to Long Crichel. Where the road swings up to the left, go straight on, into **Manor Road** following the sign towards Cashmoor. Continue along the broad green valley, passing modern houses on the left. Cross a stile by a gate into the driveway of **Manor Farm**.

At the farm turn down the drive to the right and soon bear left across a stile and along a cinder track. Follow this for a ¼ mile (400m), until you are level with a clump of trees on the left. Cross a stile to your right, then a bridge and

another stile. Bear slightly left across the field to a further stile, with the buildings of **Ryall's Lodge** to your left. Walk up the laurel hedge and bear left of the wooden shed to cross a stile into the drive. Turn right then go through a gate and continue up to meet a lane.

Turn left along this lane. Pass a house on your left and turn up a lane to your right, following the blue waymarker. Continue as the lane becomes a green track on the

---

WHILE YOU'RE THERE

The ruin of **Knowleton church**, set just off the B3078, is a curiosity well worth a visit. It sits in splendid isolation at the centre of a circular henge with a ritual significance that is now lost. A church was first erected here in Norman times, but there is no sign of the village that once accompanied it – that disappeared centuries ago, wiped out by the plague. Today the grassy bank is smothered with wild flowers and butterflies, making it a peaceful spot for a picnic.

route of an old droving road, parallel with the Dorset Cursus to your left. Pass a farm and stay on the track as it kinks left across the **Cursus** then bends right up the hill.

The Cursus is an intriguing broad track, between parallel banks and ditches, some 6 miles (9.7km) long, running across this north east corner of Dorset from Bokerley Dyke to a cluster of long barrows and tumuli. It appears to be aligned with the rising and setting sun at midsummer and midwinter. Its edges have been blurred by time and the plough, but one of the clearest sections can be seen here. It's believed to have been built in neolithic times, around 2000 BC, but for what purpose isn't clear.

> **WHERE TO EAT AND DRINK** ℹ
>
> The **Drovers Inn** at nearby Gussage All Saints has a good-sized garden and welcomes children and dogs. The interior is pleasant and airy, with light oak tables, old beams and a bright modern bar. Indulge in a Blue Vinney ploughman's, Thai fishcakes or home-baked pork pie, followed by apple strudel and custard.

At the top of **Gussage Hill** turn right on to the grassy bridleway. Follow this for about a mile (1.6km) along the ridge, with views northwards over Gussage Down. You can see the shadow of the parallel ditches of the Cursus heading away towards Pentridge and Penbury Knoll, marked by a clump of dark firs. Hollows and hummocks on the flank of Gussage Hill suggest the remains of a large neolithic settlement and the top is liberally scattered with tumuli and long barrows. Do this walk towards the end of the day and the low light of the setting sun makes the ground shimmer silver with cobwebs.

> **WHAT TO LOOK FOR** ℹ
>
> Dorset originally provided a vast acreage of unfenced grazing for sheep. These would be moved around via a network of broad, hedged **droving lanes**, many of which still exist. Often stuffed with wild flowers and sometimes overgrown, they provide ideal walking tracks today and are identified by the old names, such as Dancing Drove and Sweetbriar Lane.

Keep straight ahead at the intersection of tracks near the top of Gussage Hill, passing the trig point on your right and a ragged line of hawthorn bushes. The trees straight ahead mark the route of the Roman Ackling Dyke, a major route that can still be traced between Old Sarum (near Salisbury) and Badbury Rings. Follow the path into the trees and immediately turn right along the track, passing an unexpectedly modern memorial stone to one John Ironmonger, who died in 1986. Ackling Dyke is raised at this point, with a ditch and bank to the right. Follow the straight track down through the trees, up beside another line of trees and down again for about 1¼ miles (2km). There's a clear view on the left to the distinctive rocket shape of Horton Tower (► Walk 3).

Pass a barn and turn left into a muddy droving lane between high hedges, following a red marker. After ½ mile (800m) this swings down to the left. Follow the gravel track downhill past the buildings of **Lower Farm**, and beside an old flint wall with tile cap, to return to **Gussage St Michael** and the lay-by. Incidentally, there are two more Gussages to discover: the larger All Saints and the tiny St Andrew. The curious name derives from the Saxon words for a spring and a watercourse.

Walk 16

Kimmeridge and Ghostly Tyneham

A coastal walk by army ranges to a not-quite-deserted village.

•DISTANCE•	7½ miles (12.1km)
•MINIMUM TIME•	3hrs 30min
•ASCENT / GRADIENT•	1,165ft (355m) ▲▲▲
•LEVEL OF DIFFICULTY•	🚶🚶 🚶🚶 🚶
•PATHS•	Grassy tracks and bridlepaths, some road walking, 12 stiles
•LANDSCAPE•	Folded hills and valleys around Kimmeridge Bay
•SUGGESTED MAP•	aqua3 OS Explorer OL 15 Purbeck & South Dorset
•START / FINISH•	Grid reference: SY 918800
•DOG FRIENDLINESS•	Notices request dogs on leads in some sections; some road walking
•PARKING•	Car park (free) in old quarry north of Kimmeridge village
•PUBLIC TOILETS•	Near Marine Centre at Kimmeridge Bay and Tyneham
•NOTE•	Range walks open most weekends throughout year and during main holiday periods; call 01929 462 721 ext 4819 for further information. Keep strictly to paths, between yellow-marked posts

BACKGROUND TO THE WALK

There's a bleakness about Kimmeridge Bay which the high energy of the surfers and the cheerful picture of families on the beach, eyes down as they potter in the rock pools, can't quite dispel. Giant slabs of black rock shelving out to sea, with crumbling cliffs topped by clumps of wild cabbage, create something of this mood. The slow, steady nodding donkey-head of the oil well above a little terrace of unmistakably industrial cottages reinforces it.

Kimmeridge Coal and Oil

The story of the bay is intriguing. Iron-Age tribes spotted the potential of the band of bituminous shale that runs through Kimmeridge, polishing it up into blackstone arm rings and ornaments, and later into chair and table legs. People have have been trying to exploit it ever since. The shale, permeated with crude oil, is also known as Kimmeridge coal, but successive attempts to work it on an industrial scale seemed doomed to failure. These included alum extraction (for dyeing) in the 16th century; use of the coal to fuel a glassworks in the 17th century (it was smelly and inefficient); and use for a variety of chemical distillations, including paraffin wax and varnish, in the 19th century. And for one brief period the street lights of Paris were lit by gas extracted from the shale oil. However, nothing lasted very long. Since 1959 BP has drilled down 1,716ft (520m) below the sea, and its beam engine sucks out some 80 barrels (2,800 gallons/12,720 litres) of crude oil a day. Transported to the Wytch Farm collection point (near Corfe Castle), the oil is then pumped to Hamble, to be shipped around the world.

In contrast to Kimmeridge, just over the hill lies Tyneham, a cosy farming village clustered around its church in a glorious valley. As you get up close, however, you realise that it's uncannily neat, like a film set from the 1940s – Greer Garson's Mrs Miniver could appear at any moment. There's a spreading oak tree by the church gate; a quaint old phone box; even a village pump. The gravestones all look freshly scrubbed – no lichen here. The farmyard is swept clean and empty. The stone cottages are newly repointed, but roofless. And the church, as you enter on a chill mid-winter day, is warm! Inside is an exhibition to explain all. The villagers were asked to give up their homes in December 1943 for the 'war effort', and Tyneham became absorbed into the vast Lulworth Ranges, as part of the live firing range. It's a touching memorial, though perhaps nothing can make up for the fact that the villagers were never allowed back to their homes. Emerging again, you half expect to see soldiers popping out of the windows, but relax, you can only visit when the ranges are closed.

Walk 16

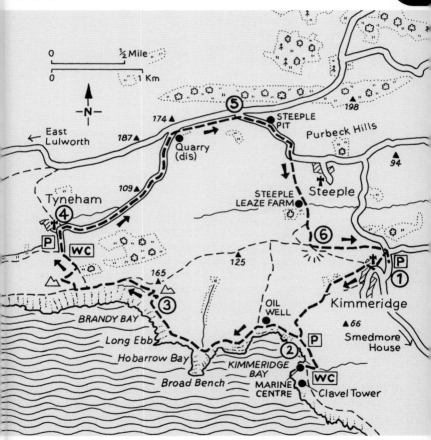

Walk 16 Directions

① Turn right up the road and soon left over a stile, signposted 'Kimmeridge' – enjoy the sweeping

views as you descend. Go through a gate by the church, then another at the bottom. Turn right past some houses, go through a gateway and bear left. Go through a gate below a coppice and soon bear left along the

Walk 16

hedge, following it round to a pair of stiles. Bear right across these and follow the path along the hedge towards the sea. Turn left on to the road, go past houses and turn right, across a car park.

② Bear left to visit the **marine centre** (closed in winter), otherwise turn right on the coastal path to continue. Descend some steps, cross a bridge and bear right, signposted 'Range Walks'. Pass some **cottages**, on the right, and the oil well. Go through the gate on to the range walk and continue around the coast on a track between yellow posts, crossing several cattle grids. The cliffs of Brandy Bay stagger away to the west.

> **WHILE YOU'RE THERE** ⓘ
> The Clavell family have been at Smedmore since the 13th century. In 1575 John Clavell was attempting to exploit the Kimmeridge shale for alum (an essential ingredient for the dyeing industry), and the current **Smedmore House**, a handsome twin-bayed affair dating from 1761, still keeps a firm eye on activities in the bay. The house is open in high summer when you can enjoy its attractive gardens, the rococo details, period furniture and a museum collection of dolls.

③ After a mile (1.6km) cross a stile and follow the path as it zig-zags sharply uphill. Continue around the top of **Brandy Bay** on the cliff path. Beside a stile and marker stone turn

down to the right, signposted 'Tyneham'. Soon cross a stile to the left and follow the track down into Tyneham village.

④ After exploring, take the exit road up the hill. At the top, by a gate, turn right over a stile and go along a path parallel with the road.

> **WHERE TO EAT AND DRINK** ⓘ
> The **post office and store** in Kimmeridge, just below the church, also doubles as a café. A favourite hang-out for surfers, it's open all day for meals and snacks, coffee, tea and drinks, and locally produced Purbeck ice cream. There's a small seating area outside and a good-sized car park.

⑤ Emerge at a gate and turn right down the road, to go past **Steeple Pit**. Where the road turns sharp left, go straight ahead down the gravel drive through **Steeple Leaze Farm** and take the gravel track ahead, leading straight up the hill. Go through a gate and keep left up a muddy path that winds through gorse and scrub, up the hill. Cross a stile at the top and continue straight ahead, with superb views over Kimmeridge.

⑥ Turn left across a stile and go straight along the edge of the field, following the ridge of the hill, for ½ mile (800m), with views to Smedmore House and Corfe Castle. Go through the gate and turn right to return to the car park.

> **WHAT TO LOOK FOR**
> Kimmeridge's unique combination of clear, shallow water, double low tides and accessible rocky ledges make it the ideal choice for a pioneering underwater nature reserve. The double low tide is at its best in the afternoons – effectively, the water may stay low all afternoon, allowing optimum access to the fingers of rock which stretch out into the bay. The low water uncovers a world of rockpools and gullies alive with seaweeds, anemones and creatures that include crabs, blennies and the bizarre pipe-fish. Learn more at the **Fine Foundation Marine Centre**.

Lawrence of Clouds Hill

Exploring the heath around the retreat of a famous British soldier.

•DISTANCE•	6 miles (9.7km)
•MINIMUM TIME•	3hrs
•ASCENT / GRADIENT•	279ft (85m) ▲▲▲
•LEVEL OF DIFFICULTY•	🚶🚶🚶
•PATHS•	Heathland tracks, forest, field and woodland paths, 9 stiles
•LANDSCAPE•	Open heath, woodland beside army training area, village
•SUGGESTED MAP•	aqua3 OS Explorer OL 15 Purbeck & South Dorset
•START / FINISH•	Grid reference: SY 825904
•DOG FRIENDLINESS•	May need lifting over some stiles due to rabbit fencing
•PARKING•	Car park on road between Bovington Camp and Clouds Hill
•PUBLIC TOILETS•	None on route

BACKGROUND TO THE WALK

The grave in Moreton churchyard is a stark slab of white marble inscribed: 'To the dear memory of T E Lawrence, Fellow of All Souls College, Oxford. Born 16 August 1888, died 19 May 1935'. It strips the romantic 'Lawrence of Arabia' legend to the bone, presenting to the world a scholar who died young. Yet the brilliant, enigmatic and haunted figure of Lawrence continues to fascinate, thanks in part to the epic film by David Lean.

Triumphant Revolt

Thomas Edward Lawrence was born in Tremadoc, North Wales. As an Oxford undergraduate he undertook a 1,100 mile (1,769km) walking tour of Palestine and Syria, collecting material for a thesis on Crusader castles. He went on to work as an archaeologist at Carchemish, Syria, and took odd jobs (such as camel driving) on wanderings throughout the Middle East and Greece. He gained a knowledge of Arab life which would prove invaluable during the First World War, when he was posted to military intelligence in Cairo. As British liaison officer to the Arab Revolt, Lawrence proved himself a leader with a driving personality and deep knowledge of strategic warfare, demonstrated in raids against the Turks. His flamboyant courage and adoption of Arabic dress made Lawrence a heroic figure, seized on by the press of the day as Akaba (Aqaba, in Jordan) was captured in 1917, and Damascus the following year.

Lawrence remained involved in Arab affairs after the war, lobbying unsuccessfully for Arab independence, and becoming increasingly frustrated. Finding fame a millstone and dissatisfied with what he described as 'the shallow grave of public duty', he joined the RAF in 1922, seeking a degree of security and regular life as Aircraftsman Ross. But he was discovered so he joined the Tank Corps at Bovington in 1923 as Private T E Shaw, and moved to Dorset, first renting and then buying the derelict house at Clouds Hill as a simple evening and weekend retreat. It is a bachelor house, surrounded by dark, high rhododendrons, with well-stocked book shelves, a gramophone, comfortable firesides and few frills. It became his 'earthly paradise'. He finished writing his account of the Arab Revolt, *The Seven Pillars of Wisdom* (1926), here, and made friends with Thomas Hardy, then living at Max Gate in Dorchester. In 1925 Lawrence rejoined the RAF, most notably spending time at Plymouth, where he helped develop and test the speedboats that formed a fledgling air-sea rescue service. In 1935 he retired to Clouds Hill. However, on 13 May of that year he went out to send a telegram. Returning quickly on his Brough Superior SS-100, he swerved to avoid two cyclists and was thrown from the motorbike. He died five days later without regaining consciousness, but his legend is still very much alive.

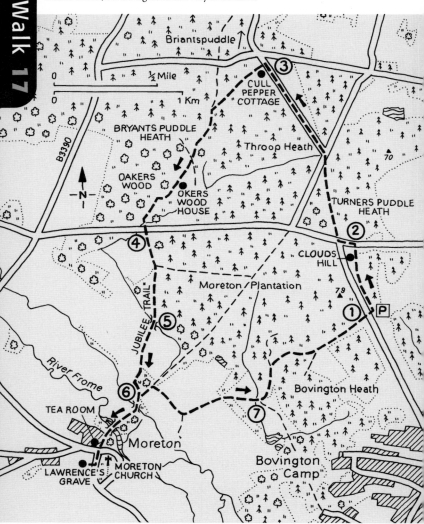

Walk 17 Directions

① Facing the back of the car park, turn left (yellow marker) along the fence through the pines. After a short distance, a stone on the left

marks where Lawrence was fatally injured. Stepping stones lead across marshy sections. The path becomes sandy and heads uphill by the fence. Rhododendrons screen **Clouds Hill**, to the left. Keep right, round the fence, then bear left to the road.

② Turn left, then at the junction cross over and turn right through a gate. Walk across **Turners Puddle Heath Nature Reserve** (a Site of Special Scientific Interest). Go through a gate at the other side and walk straight up the road ahead, signed 'Briantspuddle'.

WHILE YOU'RE THERE ⓘ

The **Tank Museum** at nearby Bovington has one of world's largest collections of armoured fighting vehicles, with exhibits from 25 countries – and you don't have to be a tank fanatic to enjoy it. The Royal Artillery, the Infantry and the Royal Armoured Corps all train their drivers on the £6 million all-weather circuit beside Clouds Hill.

---

③ After ½ mile (800m), before a junction, turn left down the path between **Cull Pepper Cottage** and its garage. Go through the gap on to a path and bear left on a firm track across **Bryants Puddle Heath**. Keep straight on at a crossing of tracks, following Hardy Way signs. Go straight on through a gate into **Oakers Wood**. Pass **Okers Wood House** and stay on the drive, which bends round to meet a road.

④ Cross the road and go straight on through more woods, with a field opening on your right. At the end of the field continue straight ahead on a woodland path. After a short distance, by an old water tank, look for the **Jubilee Trail** waymarker and turn right, walking down through the pine trees. Follow the trail as it winds through rhododendrons, later bearing right over a streambed.

⑤ Cross a pair of stiles and a footbridge at the end of the woods. Bear right across the field. Cross another footbridge and bear

diagonally right to a stile in a fence. Head straight on, cross a stile by a big trough and keep left round the edge of the next field.

⑥ Cross a stile in the corner and turn right into the lane. Go over two bridges and keep right to cross a long bridge over a ford. Pass the former post office and reach a three-way road junction (tea rooms on the right). Walk straight ahead to visit the graveyard (through a porticoed gateway) that contains Lawrence's grave. Return past the junction and turn right for **Moreton church**. Retrace your route to Point ⑥ and keep straight on. At a junction of tracks turn right and, at the end, bear left. The broad track leads past cottages into woodland and on to the heath.

WHERE TO EAT AND DRINK ⓘ

The old diamond-windowed schoolhouse in Moreton now houses the **Moreton Tearooms** They're open at lunchtime for tasty, home-made wholefood (such as spinach in filo pastry), as well as fresh sandwiches, ice creams and cold drinks.

---

⑦ Soon turn left up the sandy track. Where it divides turn right, up the hill. At the top of the hill cross the stile and turn left along the fence. Cross the stile at the end, go over the road and bear left back to the car park.

WHAT TO LOOK FOR ⓘ

Don't miss the breathtaking windows in **Moreton church**. The church itself was rebuilt after severe bomb damage in 1940. What, from the outside, looks like plain glass, from the inside is revealed engraved with a vivid flow of delicate pictorial designs. The etching is the work of Lawrence Whistler, whose first commission in 1955 led to a lifelong association with the church.

Lulworth to Durdle Door

An exhilarating walk on a spectacular piece of coastline.

•DISTANCE•	6¾ miles (10.9km)
•MINIMUM TIME•	3hrs 30min
•ASCENT / GRADIENT•	1,247ft (380m) ▲▲▲
•LEVEL OF DIFFICULTY•	然 然 然
•PATHS•	Stone path, grassy tracks, tarmac, muddy field path, 8 stiles
•LANDSCAPE•	Steeply rolling cliffs beside sea, green inland
•SUGGESTED MAP•	aqua3 OS Explorer OL 15 Purbeck & South Dorset
•START / FINISH•	Grid reference: SY 821800
•DOG FRIENDLINESS•	Excitable dogs need strict control near cliff edge
•PARKING•	Pay-and-display car park (busy), signed at Lulworth Cove
•PUBLIC TOILETS•	Beside Heritage Centre; also just above Lulworth Cove

BACKGROUND TO THE WALK

Lulworth Cove is an almost perfectly circular bay in the rolling line of cliffs that form Dorset's southern coast. Its pristine condition and geological importance earned it World Heritage status in 2002. The cove provides a secure anchorage for small fishing boats and pleasure craft, and a sun-trap of safe water for summer bathers. The cliffs around the eastern side of the bay are crumbly soft and brightly coloured in some places, while around the opposite arm the rock appears to have been folded and shoved aside by an unseen hand. The geology is intriguing and a visit to the Heritage Centre will help you to sort it out.

The oldest layer, easily identified here, is the gleaming white Portland stone. This attractive stone was much employed by Christopher Wren in his rebuilding of London. It is a fine-grained oolite, around 140 million years old. It consists of tightly compressed, fossilised shells – the flat-coiled ones are ammonites. Occasional giant ammonites, called titanites, may be seen incorporated into house walls across Purbeck. Like the rock of Bat's Head, it may contain speckled bands of flinty chert. Above this is a layer of Purbeck marble, a limestone rich in the fossils of vertebrates. This is where dinosaur, fish and reptile fossils are usually found. The soft layer above this consists of Wealden beds, a belt of colourful clays, silts and sands, that are unstable and prone to landslips when exposed.

Crumbly, white chalk overlays the Wealden beds. The chalk consists of the remains of microscopic sea creatures and shells deposited over a long period of time when a deep sea covered much of Dorset, some 75 million years ago. This is the chalk that underlies Dorset's famous downland and is seen in the exposed soft, eroded cliffs at White Nothe. Hard nodules and bands of flint appear in the chalk – it's a purer type of chert – and in its gravel beach form it protects long stretches of this fragile coast.

The laying down of chalk marks the end of the Cretaceous period in geology. After this the blanket of chalk was uplifted, folded and subjected to erosion by the slow, inexorable movement of tectonic plates. The Dorset coast was exposed to some of its most extreme pressure between 24 and 1½ million years ago, resulting in folding, crumpling and sometimes overturning of strata. You can see this in the vertical strata on rocks around Durdle Door and Stair Hole.

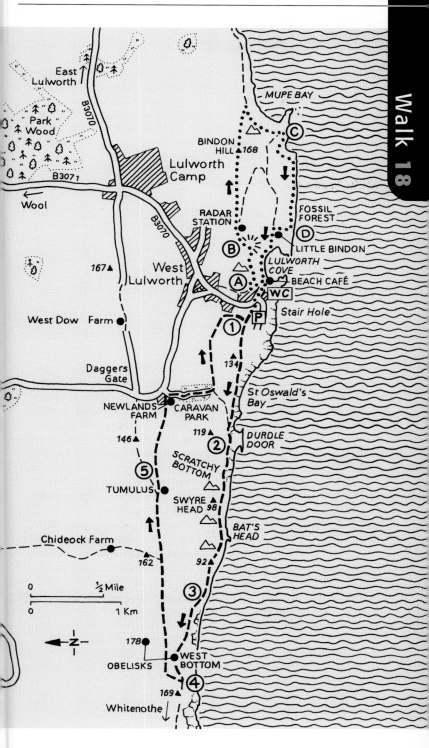

East
Lulworth

Park
Wood

B3070

B3071

Wool

MUPE BAY

BINDON
HILL ▲168

Lulworth
Camp

Lulworth
Camp

RADAR
STATION

B3070

167▲

West
Lulworth

West Dow   Farm

Daggers
Gate

Ⓒ

FOSSIL
FOREST

Ⓓ

LITTLE BINDON

LULWORTH
COVE

Ⓑ

Ⓐ

BEACH CAFÉ

WC

Stair Hole

Ⓟ

① 134▲

St Oswald's
Bay

NEWLANDS
FARM

CARAVAN
PARK

146▲

119▲

②

DURDLE
DOOR

SCRATCHY
BOTTOM

⑤

TUMULUS

SWYRE
HEAD 98▲

BAT'S
HEAD

Chideock Farm

162▲

92▲

③

0   ½ Mile

0   1 Km

←–Z–

178▲

OBELISKS

WEST
BOTTOM

169▲

④

Whitenothe

Walk 18

Walk 18 Directions

① Find a stile at the back of the car park. Cross this to take the broad, paved footpath that leads up some shallow steps to the top of the first hill. Continue along the brow, and down the other side. Pass below a **caravan park** and cross a stile.

② Reach the cove of **Durdle Door**, almost enclosed from the sea by a line of rocks. A flight of steps leads down to the sea here, but carry on walking straight ahead on the coast path and the natural stone arch of the Door itself is revealed in a second cove below you. The mass of Swyre Head looms close and yes, that is the path you're going to take, ascending straight up the side. Walk down to the bottom then climb back up to **Swyre Head**. The path leads steeply down again on the other side, to a short stretch overlooking **Bat's Head**. Climb the next steep hill. Continue along the path behind the cliffs, where the land tilts away from the sea.

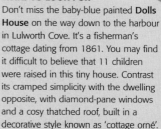

WHERE TO EAT AND DRINK
In Lulworth the **Heritage Centre café** includes family meals and baguettes. Just down the hill, the **Lulworth Cove Hotel** is open all year and serves a multitude of fresh, locally caught fish.

③ The path climbs more gently up the next hill. Pass a **navigation obelisk** on the right, and follow the path as it curves round the contour above **West Bottom**.

④ At a marker stone that indicates Whitenothe ahead turn right, over a stile, and follow a fence inland. The path curves round so you're walking parallel with the coast on level greensward. Pass three stone embrasures with shell sculptures inside, and a second obelisk. Go through a gate. Now keep straight ahead along the top of the field and across a crossing of paths, signed to Daggers Gate. Go through a gateway and straight on. The path starts to descend gently. In the next field the path becomes more of a track. Bear right to pass close by a tumulus and reach a stile.

WHAT TO LOOK FOR
Don't miss the baby-blue painted **Dolls House** on the way down to the harbour in Lulworth Cove. It's a fisherman's cottage dating from 1861. You may find it difficult to believe that 11 children were raised in this tiny house. Contrast its cramped simplicity with the dwelling opposite, with diamond-pane windows and a cosy thatched roof, built in a decorative style known as 'cottage orné'.

⑤ Cross this and walk along the top of the field, above **Scratchy Bottom**. Cross a stile into a green lane leading to **Newlands Farm**. Follow it round to the right, and turn right into the caravan park. Go straight ahead on the road through here. At the far side cross a stile and turn left, signed to West Lulworth. Stay along the field edge, cross a stile and walk above a farm lane, around the end of the hill. Keep straight on at the fingerpost and reach the stiles above the car park. Turn left and retrace your route.

WHILE YOU'RE THERE
At nearby East Lulworth is **Lulworth Castle Park**. The castle itself, a 17th-century hunting lodge built four-square with pepperpot towers, is a handsome shell, but was gutted by fire in 1929 and only partly restored. Other attractions on the estate include a circular chapel, an animal farm and an adventure playground for children.

Fossils and Mupe Bay

Take this alternative to view the geological oddity of a fossil forest.
See map and information panel for Walk 18

•DISTANCE•	4¼ miles (6.8km)
•MINIMUM TIME•	2hrs 30min
•ASCENT / GRADIENT•	617ft (188m) ▲▲▲
•LEVEL OF DIFFICULTY•	🚶 🚶 🚶
•NOTE•	Lulworth Army Ranges (► Walk 16 for advice)

Walk 19 Directions (Walk 18 option)

Two notes of caution are needed. Firstly, for walkers, the very steep descent of Bindon Hill is not for vertigo sufferers. Secondly, for dogs, running free over the firing range is dangerous, in case of unexploded shells, and, on a lighter note, the gravelly beach section at the end may be tough on soft paws.

Leave the car park by the lower entrance towards the cove. Pass a pond and turn left up the path just before the **Beach Café**, signposted 'Bindon Hill'. Steps lead up and a stone marker points you to the left, through woodland, Point Ⓐ.

Cross a stile. Bear right along a fence on a zig-zagging path. At the junction keep straight on, signposted 'Fossil Forest'. At the corner turn left up the fence, signposted 'Range Walks', Point Ⓑ.

Turn right through a gate on to the firing range. Go straight ahead up the track, past a radar station. Where the track forks keep left along the ridge of **Bindon Hill**. Cross a stile and turn right

downhill, signed 'Mupe Beach'. The path zig-zags down steeply, with steps. At the bottom take the path ahead past **Mupe Bay**, Point Ⓒ (ignoring a track leading off left down to the shore). Continue, bearing right around the point, passing the remains of a gun emplacement then a **radar station**. Below, on your left, look for the weird formations of the **Fossil Forest** in the cliffs, Point Ⓓ. Ahead steps lead down to the ledges for closer exploration.

There are no stone trees in the Fossil Forest – what you will see are stone rings where sediment has bubbled up around tree-trunks that rotted away millions of years ago. Together with the fossilised soil discovered beneath the tree boles, they give an insight into Jurassic life here, 135 million years ago.

At the flagpole turn right through a gate, signed 'Little Bindon'. Go down the gravel track. At the second flagpole turn left through a gate. Follow the path past the deserted farm of **Little Bindon**. At the end turn left and go down steps on to the shore of **Lulworth Cove**. Turn right to walk along the shingle. Turn right again by the **café** to return to the car park.

Walk 20

The Martyrs of Tolpuddle

From the village of heroes into a peaceful, secretive valley.

•DISTANCE•	4½ miles (7.2km)
•MINIMUM TIME•	2hrs 30min
•ASCENT / GRADIENT•	394ft (120m) ▲▲▲
•LEVEL OF DIFFICULTY•	󰀀󰀀󰀀
•PATHS•	Village roads, farm tracks, rocky footpath, bridlepaths, 1 stile
•LANDSCAPE•	Gently rolling farmland above valley of River Piddle
•SUGGESTED MAP•	aqua3 OS Explorer 117 Cerne Abbas & Bere Regis
•START / FINISH•	Grid reference: SY 787945
•DOG FRIENDLINESS•	Some road walking
•PARKING•	Lay-by beside Martyrs Museum; or on high street
•PUBLIC TOILETS•	None on route

Walk 20 Directions

From the **Martyrs Museum** head towards the centre of the village. Pass a row of houses and turn up to the left, signposted 'Dewlish', on a lane which hooks back behind the same houses. Continue up a path through scrubby woodland, towards the bypass. It's a noisy but necessary evil, freeing the village of traffic, and the path detours to cross it. So, at the top turn right through the gate, go down the track beside the bypass and turn left through the

---

WHAT TO LOOK FOR ℹ

The Martyrs' Tree in the heart of Tolpuddle is the source of the village's fame. It was a meeting point for the Friendly Society of Agricultural Labourers, a group that had been formed to peaceably press their masters for better pay. At that time a local labourer's wage was just 7 shillings a week – around 3 shillings below what was paid elsewhere in Dorset. The six, picked out as trouble makers, were George and James Loveless, Thomas and John Standfield, James Brine and James Hammett.

---

underpass. At the other side turn immediately left through a gate and walk to the end. Turn right here, through a gate. Bear diagonally left across the field, climbing steadily up to a plateau.

Tolpuddle is tucked down in a fold of hill behind you, already invisible. This sleepy Dorset village entered the history books in 1834 when six of its farm labourers became known as the Tolpuddle Martyrs. They were among the 1,800 individuals, convicted of political crimes, who were shipped out to Australia between 1800 and 1850. These 'dangerous elements' were effectively silenced by being sent to another, apparently God-forsaken world. They included Luddites and rioters, Chartists and radicals. The case of the Tolpuddle Martyrs was unusual. They had been convicted at Dorchester of 'administering unlawful oaths'. In fact the men had illegally banded together to press for improved pay and conditions at a time when many in England were starving. Their sentences were eventually quashed after public

---

WHERE TO EAT AND DRINK ⓘ

Tolpuddle's friendly **Martyrs' Inn** is open all day and serves a tasty range of pub food from lunchtime, including baguettes and fish and chips. Children are welcome in the pub and restaurant, dogs in the public bar area. The pub doubles as a West Dorset Tourist Information point.

---

outrage, and the men were pardoned. Still, it took five years to bring them all home.

Go through a gateway and continue straight on beside a thick hawthorn hedge, through another gateway and over the top of the hill. The gentle folds of **Burleston Down** are to your left. Continue down the other side but bear right before the corner of the field through an old, broken gate, to walk down a narrow track between high banks and trees. The path levels out. Turn right through a gap in the hedge, with a hedge to your immediate left (there is a blue marker, but it's behind you), and keep straight on along the bridleway. Look out for deer on the big sweep of chalk downland up to your right. Pass some derelict barns on the left. At the corner of the field go right, over the fence, and straight along the bottom of a secret green valley. Go through a gate. The radio transmission mast on Warren Hill is up to the right. Cross a stile by a gate and go on through another gate. Pass an area of scrubby woodland on the left. In front of you, almost blocking the end of the valley, is the magnificent **Weatherby Castle**, a rampart-ringed fort covered in trees.

The track rises to meet a wooden gate. Go through and turn up to the right, to meet a rough gravel road that leads up the hill, leaving the castle on your left. The main track swings right through a gateway – ignore this, and stay straight ahead up the hill. Go through a gate in the narrow, top corner, into a green lane through trees.

Go through a gate at the far end and continue along the top of the field over the crest of the hill, with a hedge on your right. Keep on through two more gates, towards the bypass. The track starts to descend by a small conifer plantation. Go through a gate and on through the farmyard. A gate at the other side leads you up over a bridge, crossing the bypass. Continue straight down the metalled road to emerge on the high street of Tolpuddle, beside the **Martyrs' Inn**.

Turn right and walk back towards the museum, passing the **Martyrs' Tree** on the triangular green, and cottages called **Little Noddings** and **Sweet William**. Outside the Martyrs Museum is a statue of one of the men, George Loveless. He was an eloquent Methodist lay preacher. He had developed a taste for life beyond these little valleys, and he emigrated to Ontario, Canada with four of the others. The only one to live out his life in the village was James Hammet. Cross over to enter the churchyard and walk through to visit his grave. Leave the churchyard via a little wooden gate and return along the high street to your car.

WHILE YOU'RE THERE ⓘ

Just down the road is **Athelhampton**, one of England's most majestic old mansions. Parts of it date from 1485. The house is stuffed with treasures, from Tudor architecture in the Great Hall to a carved Charles I tester bed. Allow time to explore the world-famous gardens with their yew topiary and fountains.

Roaming the Woods at Ashmore

A gentle amble through plantations of mixed woodland to a village highpoint.

•DISTANCE•	5¾ miles (9.2km)
•MINIMUM TIME•	3hrs
•ASCENT / GRADIENT•	427ft (130m)
•LEVEL OF DIFFICULTY•	
•PATHS•	Forestry and farm tracks, woodland and field paths, 1 stile
•LANDSCAPE•	Mixed woodland, quiet village
•SUGGESTED MAP•	aqua3 OS Explorer 118 Shaftesbury & Cranborne Chase
•START / FINISH•	Grid reference: ST 897167
•DOG FRIENDLINESS•	One short stretch of road walking
•PARKING•	At Washers Pit entrance to Ashmore Wood
•PUBLIC TOILETS•	None on route

BACKGROUND TO THE WALK

To anyone familiar with the monotonous, sterile conifer forests of northern Britain, the plantations of Dorset are a revelation and a delight. Best among these are the Forestry Commission's woods around Ashmore. At the time of the Domesday Book around 15 per cent of the land area of England was covered by woodland. A survey undertaken in 2000 put that figure at 8.4 per cent, with oak accounting for a quarter of all broadleaved trees.

Timber Target
The Forestry Commission was set up as a Government body in 1919, partly in response to the timber shortage created by the needs of booming industry in the 18th and 19th centuries. Furthermore, timber shortage had been identified as a critical problem during the First World War. Not only was it required for making pit props for coal mines but trench warfare also swallowed up vast quantities of timber for shoring up and lining the trenches. The Commission's early brief – to grow as much timber as possible in as short a time as possible – has changed over the years. Nowadays, sensitivity to local soil conditions, conservation and the needs of wildlife and public access for leisure also play a part in the choice of how a woodland is created and managed, and what is planted.

Ashmore Wood has the feel of a showpiece forest. As you walk down its broad tracks you'll notice an appealing variety of smaller tree species planted along the margins and plenty of bird nesting boxes in evidence. Although obviously plantation woodland, it represents replanting on the site of much older woods. Ashmore is therefore rich in wild flowers, especially bluebells in late spring, but also celandines, primroses and the tall spears of great mullein and foxgloves. The forestry planting is a combination of broadleaved woodland and mixed conifers. The beeches, magnificent in their autumn colour, stifle most things growing in the shade at their feet, but harbour the best sites for fungi. Beneath the conifers emerald moss grows in pillowy mounds, creating a sparkling fairyland in the filtered sunlight.

Ashmore village is the highest in Dorset and stands on the border with Wiltshire. Thatched houses cluster around a large circular duckpond. The village is on the road to nowhere in particular and has no pub (although a discreet stone carving over a doorway suggests there was a Stag's Head here not too long ago). Ashmore has remained pleasantly uncommercialised and feels like a discovery. The greenish tinge that gives an old-fashioned air to its houses is from the colour of the local sandstone. Spare a glance for the corbelled end wall of Manor Farm, which may have been lifted from Eastbury Hall (▶ Walk 14).

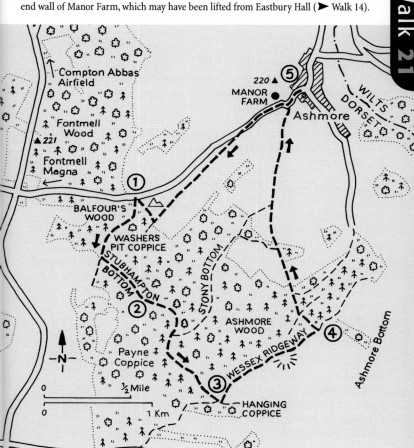

Walk 21 Directions

① With your back to the road, walk past the gate and follow the firm forestry road as it curves past the beeches of **Washers Pit Coppice** on your left and **Balfour's Wood** on your right. After ½ mile (800m) ignore a crossing bridleway and stay straight ahead on the track. You're now in **Stubhampton Bottom**, following a quiet winding valley through the trees.

② Where the main track swings up to the left, keep straight ahead, following the blue public bridleway marker, on a rutted track along the valley floor. A path from **Stony Bottom** feeds in from the left – keep straight on. Where an area of

Walk 21

exposed hillside appears on the left, follow the blue markers on to the narrower track to the right, which runs down through coppiced woodland parallel and below the forestry road. At **Hanging Coppice** a fingerpost shows where the Wessex Ridgeway path feeds in from the right – again, keep straight ahead. The path soon rises to emerge at the corner of a field.

③ Turn left at the fence (following the blue marker) to walk uphill. Follow this path along the edge of the forest, with good views to the south east of low rolling hills and secretive valleys.

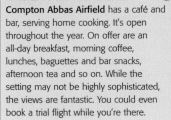

> **WHERE TO EAT AND DRINK** ⓘ
>
> **Compton Abbas Airfield** has a café and bar, serving home cooking. It's open throughout the year. On offer are an all-day breakfast, morning coffee, lunches, baguettes and bar snacks, afternoon tea and so on. While the setting may not be highly sophisticated, the views are fantastic. You could even book a trial flight while you're there.

> **WHILE YOU'RE THERE** ⓘ
>
> Drive down into the pretty village of **Fontmell Magna**, along an attractive route that brings you in past a big duck pond. A sign on your left by a little bridge marks the shallow sheep wash in the stream. This was used for washing sheep until modern dips came along in the 1930s. Just beyond the Crown pub, the Fontmell Potteries recalls that this was a centre of terracotta making.

④ After ¾ mile (1.2km) turn left at a marked junction of tracks and walk through the woods. Cross over a track and keep straight on, following the blue marker, to meet a track. Go straight on, following signs for the **Wessex Ridgeway**, and passing under a large beech tree. Go through an old gate. Next, continue straight up this track for about 1 mile (1.6km), through farmland and across the exposed open hilltop, with the houses of **Ashmore** village appearing. At the end of the track turn right and walk into the village to the duck pond.

⑤ Retrace your route but stay on the road out of the village, passing

Manor Farm on the right and heading gently downhill. Just before the road narrows to single track width, bear left through a gate (blue marker). Walk along the top of the field, pass a gate on the left and bear slightly down to the right to reach the lower of two gates at the far side. Cross the stile and walk straight ahead on a broad green track. Go through a gate into the woods and immediately turn right, following a steep bridleway straight down the side of the hill to emerge by the car park.

> **WHAT TO LOOK FOR** ⓘ
>
> Opposite the pond in Ashmore, the **war memorial cross** records the names of local members of the Dorset Regiment and Dorset Yeomanry who died in the First World War. There is just one addition to the roll for the Second World War: G Coombs, a pilot with the South African Air Force (SAAF), who died in 1942.

Melbury Hill and Fontmell Down

Over the preserved downs around Compton Abbas, in search of butterflies and wild flowers.

•DISTANCE•	4½ miles (7.2km)
•MINIMUM TIME•	2hrs
•ASCENT / GRADIENT•	820ft (250m)
•LEVEL OF DIFFICULTY•	
•PATHS•	Downland tracks, muddy bridleway, village lanes, 3 stiles
•LANDSCAPE•	Rolling downland with superb views
•SUGGESTED MAP•	aqua3 OS Explorer 118 Shaftesbury & Cranborne Chase
•START / FINISH•	Grid reference: ST 886187
•DOG FRIENDLINESS•	Some road walking
•PARKING•	Car park on road south of Shaftesbury, near Compton Abbas Airfield
•PUBLIC TOILETS•	None on route

BACKGROUND TO THE WALK

Since the end of the Second World War over 80 per cent of the chalk downs in England have been altered or lost because enriching artificial fertilisers have been introduced and land has been claimed for arable crops. Grazing is the key, in a scheme first introduced by the neolithic farmers. Without grazing, the close-cropped grass of the downs would soon revert to scrub and woodland. Modern management is therefore based on restoring the old farming cycles of grazing by sheep and cattle and maintaining the land for the benefit of threatened wildlife as well as for agricultural output. Preservation of the precious habitat of the outstanding area of Melbury and Fontmell Downs is in the hands of the National Trust with assistance from the Dorset Wildlife Trust.

Beautiful Butterflies

A chief beneficiary of this policy is the butterfly, for more than 35 species have been recorded here. Some have very specific requirements for their survival. The silver spotted skipper, for example, breeds in only 14 places in Britain, and only one in Dorset – Fontmell Down. They lay their eggs on the underside of sheep's fescue grass, but the grass has to be just the right length. If the juicy new grass shoots are nibbled by the sheep in August, the caterpillars will starve. Adonis blues are hardly less demanding – they need a tightly packed, south-facing, warm grassy slope. The grand-sounding Duke of Burgundy fritillary, on the other hand, likes to live on the edge – the edge of the sward, that is, where the cowslips blossom in springtime. (This need for a bit of rough may be a betrayal of its origin as the more humble 'Mr Vernon's small fritillary', for it was renamed in the 18th century.)

Wild Flowers

The wealth and variety of wild flowers found on these chalky downs is, of course, the other delight. They bloom unmolested, thriving on the poorer soils, not squeezed out by faster-growing monocultures. In summer look for the vivid violet-blue specks of early gentians in the turf, the tiny stalked spikes of the mauve milkwort and the deeper purple of thyme. They give way in autumn to the browny yellow flowers of the carline thistle and the spiralling, white-flowered spikes of autumn lady's tresses.

In autumn, this is a place to find glow-worms. About the length of a fingernail, these little creatures were once a common sight. It is the females who glow. Wingless and defenceless, they hide during the day, but at night crawl on to vegetation to shine their lower abdomens upwards to attract males flying by. The intense green pinpoint of light is caused by oxyluciferin, manufactured by specially adapted body cells which combine oxygen, water and an enzyme to emit light without generating heat.

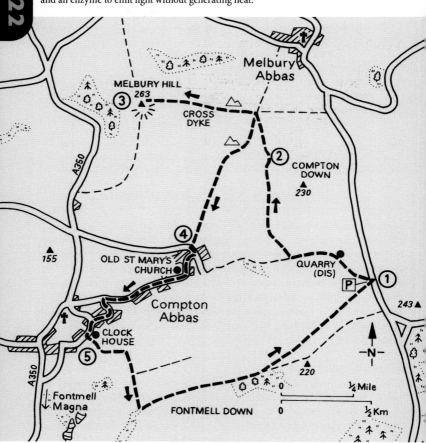

Walk 22 Directions

① Take the rough track from the bottom right corner of the car park, walking downhill towards **Compton Abbas**. Pass an old chalk quarry and continue downhill.

Soon turn right up some wooden steps and cross a stile to access **Compton Down**. Bear left and uphill towards a fence. Follow a track that contours round, just below the top of the hill, heading towards the saddle between the down and **Melbury Hill**.

Walk 22

② Pass a steep, natural amphitheatre on your left, go across the saddle and turn left at the fence. Follow this to the top of **Melbury Hill** – a steep climb but well worth it for the views. Pass the scar of an ancient cross dyke, on the left as you climb, and look down the other side to the silvery tower of Melbury Abbas church.

> **WHILE YOU'RE THERE**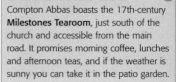
> Just east of here, over the border in Wiltshire, **Win Green Hill** (another National Trust property) is crowned by a ring of trees. It's the highest point of the ancient royal forest of Cranborne Chase (▶ Walk 11), and the views are superb. When he tired of the hunt, King John hung out at nearby Tollard Royal.

③ A trig point marks the top of the hill, with fantastic views all around, including Shaftesbury on its ridge to the north (▶ Walk 25) and the ridges of Hambledon Hill to the south east (▶ Walk 23). Retrace your route downhill, with views over Melbury Down and to Compton Abbas Airfield. Turn right on to the farm track. After a short distance bear left, down a steep path, to a gate. Go through this and

> **WHAT TO LOOK FOR**
> As you walk towards Compton Abbas, pause at the churchyard of old **St Mary's**. Rest a moment on the great mounting block by the wall, to admire the ancient farmhouse opposite. All that remains of the old church is the ghostly, pale tower, blocked up and left to the pigeons. In the graveyard itself are some crumbling tombs and the weathered stump of an old cross. A new St Mary's was built within the village in 1866.

> **WHERE TO EAT AND DRINK**
> Compton Abbas boasts the 17th-century **Milestones Tearoom**, just south of the church and accessible from the main road. It promises morning coffee, lunches and afternoon teas, and if the weather is sunny you can take it in the patio garden.

bear immediately left through a second gate. Go straight along the muddy field edge towards Compton Abbas. Pass through a gate and emerge on to a road.

④ Turn left and follow this road right round a sharp bend. Pass the tower of the original church, isolated in its small graveyard. Continue along the lane, passing houses of varying ages, with the spire of the modern church ahead in the trees. Descend between high hedges and turn left at the junction. Continue on this winding road through the bottom of the village, passing attractive, stone-built, thatched cottages.

⑤ Pass **Clock House** and turn left up the bridleway, signposted 'Gore Clump'. The gravel track gives way to a tree-lined lane between the fields. Go through a gate and continue straight on. Cross a stile by a gate and continue ahead along the edge of a field. In the corner, turn left along a fence and walk up the track above some trees to reach a gate. Pass through this on to **Fontmell Down**. Continue straight ahead on the rising track. After ½ mile (800m) ignore the stile to the right and keep straight ahead along the fence, to reach the top of the hill and a stile into the car park.

Exploring Hambledon Hill

Take the gentle route up a famous sculpted landmark.

•DISTANCE•	4½ miles (7.2km)
•MINIMUM TIME•	3hrs
•ASCENT / GRADIENT•	541ft (165m)
•LEVEL OF DIFFICULTY•	
•PATHS•	Village, green and muddy lanes, bridleways, hillside, 6 stiles
•LANDSCAPE•	Pastoral, dominated by Hambledon Hill, outstanding views
•SUGGESTED MAP•	aqua3 OS Explorer 118 Shaftesbury & Cranborne Chase
•START / FINISH•	Grid reference: ST 860124
•DOG FRIENDLINESS•	Good but some road walking
•PARKING•	Lay-by opposite Church of St Mary's
•PUBLIC TOILETS•	None on route

BACKGROUND TO THE WALK

The locals would have you believe that you can see America from the top of Hambledon Hill. That's perhaps a little optimistic, but the New World link is not entirely spurious. Lieutenant Colonel (later General) James Wolfe trained his troops here for ten weeks in 1756. Wolfe was already a veteran of the Jacobite Rebellion in Scotland. All that yomping the steep hillsides must have been worth it, for three years later his troops would scale the cliffs of the Heights of Abraham and capture Quebec – and Canada – for the British. (Wolfe himself was mortally wounded in the battle.)

An Iron-Age Community
The ditches and ramparts of a fort that dates from the Iron Age encircle the top of Hambledon Hill, giving it a profile that can be recognised from miles around. Today it is acknowledged as a site of international importance for the quality of its rare downland and its archaeology. The platforms of 200 huts have been discovered within the ramparts of the fort, offering a glimpse of how our ancestors lived – it is strange to think of this high, peaceful spot occupied by an entire community.

Such a distinctive landmark as Hambledon Hill was a natural choice for a rallying of serious-minded folk in 1645. They were the local branch of the Dorset Clubmen, ordinary people for the most part who were heartily sick of the Civil War, and particularly of losing out by being caught in the middle of plundering troops from both sides. Their idea was to declare Dorset a neutral zone until the King and Parliament had sorted out their differences – preferably somewhere else. The King, soundly defeated at the Battle of Naseby earlier in the year, was supportive of the movement. However, to Oliver Cromwell and his fellow commander Thomas Fairfax, it represented a dangerous and obstructive nuisance. When the Clubmen, determined not to be overlooked, tried to cut off Fairfax's supplies as he swept through North Dorset, he seized and imprisoned their ringleaders at Shaftesbury.

Home Defeat
On 4 August some 4,000 angry and ill-armed Clubmen then faced Cromwell and the horsemen of his New Model Army on Hambledon Hill. They suffered a humiliating defeat

on their home ground. Around 60 of their number were killed (some accounts say only 12), and around 300 were taken prisoner, including no less than four rectors and their curates. Cromwell locked them up in Shroton church overnight. They were allowed home the next day, after promising not to do it again. After this, the Dorset Clubmen disappeared from history. The Parliamentary army stormed on to take Sherborne Castle a few days later, another decisive step towards their eventual victory.

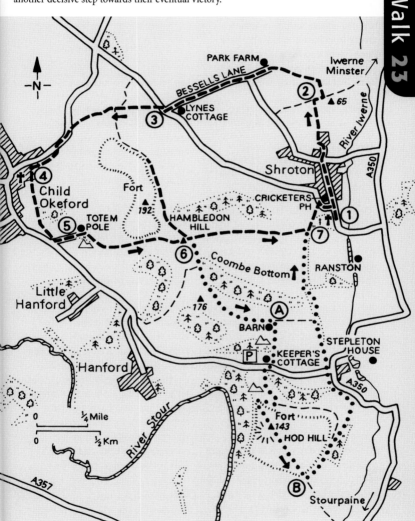

Walk 23 Directions

① With the church on your left, walk up the street. Pass a farmhouse on the corner of **Main Street** and

Frog Lane. Note behind you the carved stone cross, placed in 2000 on the stump of an old cross. Cross the road into the lane opposite, signed to Courteney Close. Pass a converted chapel, fork left and go through a gate. Keep right along the hedge. Where the gardens end keep straight ahead through a gate and across a field.

② Turn right when you reach the fence, cross a stile and turn left. Go through a gate and bear left up a grassy lane between hedges. Pass **Park Farm** and keep straight ahead. At the junction bear right into **Bessells Lane**.

WHILE YOU'RE THERE ⓘ

Call in at the neighbouring village of **Iwerne Minster** to admire the church, which dates from the 14th century. Its elegant spire can be seen from the walk. In fact, it is one of only three medieval spires in Dorset. When first built it was apparently twice as tall – restoration in the 19th century cut it down to size.

---

③ At the end, by **Lynes Cottage**, bear right and immediately left up a muddy bridleway, with a line of trees to your left. At the top go through a gate and bear left down a narrow lane, part of a defensive ditch at the foot of the hill. At the road turn left and head into **Child Okeford**. Just past the post box turn left and cross a stile. Bear right along the edge of the park, towards the church tower. When you get to the fence turn left.

④ Cross the drive and keep straight on, with glimpses of the chimneys of the Victorian manor house to the left. At the corner cross a stile and keep straight ahead down a path. Cross a stone stile by the road and immediately turn left up a lane. This becomes a track, climbing steeply through trees.

⑤ Pass a millennium **totem pole** and follow the lane right and uphill. Go through a gate and keep straight

---

WHERE TO EAT AND DRINK ⓘ

The **Cricketers** in Shroton is a cosy place, with a set of cricket stumps stuck on the front door in case you're feeling your way in. Walkers are requested to leave their muddy boots outside. Dogs are welcome in the beer garden to one side, children inside. As well as standard bar meals, the smart restaurant's inventive menu list includes black pudding with a mustard cream sauce and chicken with maple barbecue sauce.

---

on up. The path levels out below the earthworks that ring the top of the hill. Go through a gate, emerge from the track and go straight on up the hill, through a gate and across the bridleway.

⑥ At the trig point turn left to explore the ancient settlement. (Turn right for Walk 24.) Return to the trig point, turn left over the top of the hill and go down the slope, following the bridleway.

⑦ Meet a track by a wall at the bottom. (Walk 24 rejoins here.) Turn left and go through a gate, with the village ahead. Follow the track down to a cricket pavilion. Go through the gate and turn right, on to the road. Follow this down past a **thatched barn** and turn right to return to your car. Alternatively, turn left at the pavilion, and soon turn right by **Hill View Cottage**, to the pub.

WHAT TO LOOK FOR ⓘ

Elizabeth Taylor married Thomas Freke, and is remembered as the 17th-century benefactress of the school in Shroton, now the village hall. Their over-the-top **chapel** within St Mary's Church was erected by their sons in 1654. Dazzling with its crests and armorial bearings, even the church's own guidebook describes it as pompous and florid.

A Short Hop to Hod Hill

Extend Walk 23 with a steep ascent to an ancient fort.
See map and information panel for Walk 3

•DISTANCE•	7½ miles (12.1km)
•MINIMUM TIME•	5hrs
•ASCENT / GRADIENT•	781ft (238m)
•LEVEL OF DIFFICULTY•	

Walk 24 **Directions** (Walk 23 option)

The detour to Hod Hill, the flat-topped hill to the south with its dramatic square-cut ramparts, rewards the effort.

At the trig point (Point ⑥) turn right and follow the track southwards. Soon there are good views of Hod Hill ahead. Go through a gate to follow a broad track round the wood. You can see flint in the chalk where the edge of the path is eroded. Continue through a field gate and look left, down to the handsome, square, Palladian **Ranston House**. The path now heads steadily downhill.

Climb a stile by the gate beside a barn (Point Ⓐ). Turn right, following the chalky track straight down the steep hill. At the bottom go through a gate and emerge on the road by **Keeper's Cottage**. Cross over and go up the track opposite. Cross a stile and follow the path that climbs straight ahead, up the steep side of **Hod Hill**. At the fence turn right and walk around the hill to the gateway and stile in to the fort. Cross through the high ramparts that encircle the hilltop to enter the fort. The Romans occupied a site already defended by great ramparts and ditches – their fort sits in one corner of the hilltop, and you walk through more ramparts to get into it. Follow the path that runs diagonally, straight across the top, with good views to Stourpaine village below.

Turn left just before the gate on the opposite side (Point Ⓑ), to walk along the outside of the ramparts. Go through a gate on the right, then turn left on to the broad chalky track that runs along the top of the woods. Follow this down the hill to reach a gate at the bottom. Take the bridleway to the left of this, walking parallel with the road for a short distance. Go through a gate and keep right, down the edge. At the corner go through a small gate, cross the road and go through a gate opposite. Walk straight up the edge of the field, with views of the old walled gardens of **Stepleton House**. Bear right, through a gate on to a track through the woods. Go through another gate, along the top of the woods and keep straight on, with the railings of **Ranston Park** on your right. The path becomes a wide, muddy track leading up beside the trees and the fence on your right gives way to a wall. Rejoin Walk 23 at Point ⑦.

Walk 25

On Top of Gold Hill

Around the streets of Shaftesbury, familiar to millions.

•DISTANCE•	3 miles (4.8km)
•MINIMUM TIME•	2hrs
•ASCENT / GRADIENT•	322ft (98m)
•LEVEL OF DIFFICULTY•	
•PATHS•	Town pavements, steep cobbles, quiet lanes, 3 stiles
•LANDSCAPE•	Town and far-reaching, pastoral views
•SUGGESTED MAP•	aqua3 OS Explorer 118 Shaftesbury & Cranborne Chase; tourist information centre has good town centre maps
•START / FINISH•	Grid reference: ST 862230
•DOG FRIENDLINESS•	Town centre not good for dogs (lots of road walking)
•PARKING•	Several car parks around town centre
•PUBLIC TOILETS•	At all town centre car parks

Walk 25 Directions

From the tourist information centre on **Bell Street** turn left, down the road. Walk past a row of terraced houses, built with stone below, brick above and thatch on top. Turn right, down **Mustons Lane**. Pass a Palladian former church on the left, now a restaurant. At the **High Street** turn right.

The town of Shaftesbury was founded by the Saxons. In medieval times it became an important pilgrimage site. In later centuries it was a centre for button making and served as a coaching stop on the main route to the West Country.

The High Street broadens into a market square by the **Mitre** pub, with medieval **St Peter's Church** and the **Town Hall**. Ahead is an attractively jumbled line of shops and houses. Walk up to the end, cross at the zebra crossing by **King Alfred's Restaurant**, and hook back down to the left. Go down the narrow lane beside the Town Hall and between the houses and you'll suddenly find yourself at the top of **Gold Hill**, with the line of cottages tipping down the steep, cobbled road ahead, and a perfect view of the green Dorset hills behind. At the top is the **Town Museum**. The view is only slightly marred by a giant fibreglass loaf, testimony to the restoration of the street in 1980.

The massive, buttressed grey walls of **Shaftesbury Abbey** stand opposite the houses on Gold Hill. Walk down the hill – it is genuinely charming, if hard on the knees – to

---

WHAT TO LOOK FOR

If you remember the 1970s then you will probably recognise Shaftesbury's **Gold Hill**. 'The Hovis advert' – a veritable classic among television commercials – which employed an extract from Dvorak's emotive *New World Symphony*, was shot here. The hill today apparently looks exactly as it did when filmed – that it does is thanks to the bread company, which contributed many thousands of pounds for the hill's restoration.

Walk 25

James Street. Turn left and follow the road along the contour of the hill. After almost ½ mile (800m) pass the junction with **French Mill Lane** and continue ahead, up **Hawkesdene Lane**. At the top turn right and cross the stile to enter the quaintly named **Wilderness Park**. Follow the grassy path above the trees and down, with Melbury Hill dominating the view to the right. Cross the stile at the end and turn immediately right, along the edge of the field. Cross another stile then turn left down the narrow lane. Continue down the hill between steep banks, passing **French Mill Cottage** on the right.

At **Three Ways Cottage** turn right. Pass a turning to **Gears Mill** and follow the road as it climbs steadily back up to the town, the horizon punctuated by the three square church towers of St Peter's, Holy Trinity and St James's. Pass **Holyrood Farm** on the left, and keep straight on up the hill. Just after a post box, and before a road junction, take the steep and uneven footpath down to the left. The path rises and becomes broad **Kingsman Lane**, a road between houses. At the top turn left on to **James Street**, tightly-packed with terraced cottages. Pass **Ye Olde Two Brewers Inn** on the left and pause to admire the **Pump Yard** on the right.

Turn right, up **Tanyard Lane**. At the top turn right by some garages. Almost immediately turn left up a cobbled path by house No 3. This steep path leads up to the top of the town, and the views improve as you climb. Steps lead on to a tarmac path, with a well-placed bench. At the top turn your back on the view and go through a small gate in the wall. Turn left along **Love Lane** and

> ### WHERE TO EAT AND DRINK
> Shaftesbury offers plenty of choice. Two recommended stops on the route are the **Salt Cellar restaurant** at the top of Gold Hill, where you can sit outside and admire the famous view, and **Ye Olde Two Brewers Inn** which welcomes families and is highly praised for its home-cooked food.

take the first path up to the right between houses, called **Langford Lane**. At the end turn right. Cross the road then, just beyond the ambulance station, turn left down a path, signposted 'Castle Views'. This leads to a vantage point with superb views out to the north. You will see as far as Glastonbury Tor on a good day. Return to the main road and turn left, passing **Ox House**. Cross back then turn right, down **Abbey Walk**, passing an old pump on the corner. Pass the curious **Old School House** on the left and turn left at the war memorial. Pass the entrance to the abbey ruins.

At the end of the walkway keep left, to emerge by a wonderful, old-fashioned confectioner's shop and the King Alfred Restaurant. Bear left, cross at the zebra crossing and keep left, passing the Georgian **Grosvenor Hotel**. Keep right, into **Bell Street** to return to the tourist information centre.

> ### WHILE YOU'RE THERE
>
> King Alfred founded a nunnery here in AD 888. The young King Edward the Martyr (▶ Walk 8) was reburied here in AD 979. **Shaftesbury Abbey** became a significant and very wealthy place of pilgrimage. The abbey was dismantled in 1539, a victim of Henry VIII's Dissolution of the monasteries. The ruins were uncovered in 1861 and now there is a garden and museum on the site, open through the summer.

Child Okeford and Mysterious Hammoon

A loop around the River Stour linking two ancient villages.

•DISTANCE•	4¼ miles (6.8km)
•MINIMUM TIME•	2hrs
•ASCENT / GRADIENT•	98ft (30m) ▲▲▲
•LEVEL OF DIFFICULTY•	🚶🚶 🚶🚶 🚶🚶
•PATHS•	Field boundaries, grassy tracks, firm road, grassy bridleways, 15 stiles
•LANDSCAPE•	Open farmland, dominated by Hambledon Hill
•SUGGESTED MAP•	aqua3 OS Explorer 129 Yeovil & Sherborne
•START / FINISH•	Grid reference: ST 822120
•DOG FRIENDLINESS•	Some unfriendly stiles
•PARKING•	Lay-by on Hayward Lane by old brick railway bridge
•PUBLIC TOILETS•	None on route

BACKGROUND TO THE WALK

Child Okeford and Hammoon are just two of the mysterious names of the villages around the green meadows of the Stour Valley. Child Okeford, huddled in the shadow of Hambledon Hill (➤ Walk 23) is one of a triumvirate of Okefords. To the south lies pretty Okeford Fitzpaine (➤ Walk 30), and the nearby quarrying village of Shillingstone was known as Shilling Okeford in the days when it boasted the highest maypole in the country.

Hammoon

Hammoon sounds faintly Eastern and romantic. In fact, the name comes from William de Moion, a Norman nobleman who was rewarded after the Conquest with a section of low-lying meadowland (or 'hamm'). The family name was later spelt Mohun (which became the 'moon' element of Moonfleet, ➤ Walk 40). The hamlet of golden brown stone buildings that is clustered round the stump of an old cross is still called Hammoon. It appears on the map as little more than a handful of farms and houses built on a meander of the river (and so liable to flooding), but there is more to Hammoon than meets the eye. Tucked behind the church, the venerable Manor Farm is particularly appealing, with tiny windows cut into the deep thatch of its roof and the 17th-century addition of a magnificently carved classical porch complete with grand columns.

Hybrid St Paul's

Next door to Manor Farm is the charming little Church of St Paul's, topped with a weathered, wooden bellcote. Step through the massive oak door to discover a harmonious interior that is not quite what it seems. Fragments of 13th-century flooring are preserved under the bell tower, but the church is probably another century older still. Some of its fittings have come from far and wide. The deeply carved reredos (the screen behind the altar) dates from the late 14th or early 15th century. It was discovered languishing in a builder's yard in London and was installed here in 1946, as part of a significant restoration

Walk 26

programme. Another improvement at that time was the addition of the lovely 16th-century choir stalls, carved with flowing vines and grapes – these came from East Anglia.

Dead Surprising

There's one more surprise on this walk. Ham Down Woodland Burial Ground is on the site of a former vineyard. It is a 'green' burial place in all senses of the word. There are no denominational barriers in this peaceful spot and no weeping statues. Coffins and memorial plaques are required to be strictly biodegradable and your loved one's grave or scattering place can be marked with the planting of a tree (of an appropriate species for the locality) and a flush of spring bulbs.

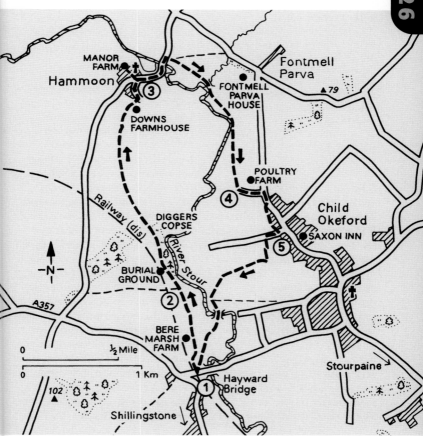

Walk 26 Directions

① Go through the gate and follow blue markers up the farm road, passing **Bere Marsh Farm**. Pass a house on the left and go straight on through a gate.

② Where the road swings left stay straight ahead. Bear to the right of the **burial ground**, down a broad, grassy ride. Follow this bridleway (blue markers) straight across the fields for a mile (1.6km) to Hammoon. You will pass **Diggers Copse** on the right and, initially, the bridleway is parallel with the route of a former railway on the left. After the sixth gate pass **Downs Farmhouse**. The track becomes a road. Bend left then right to emerge opposite the stump of an ancient cross. Cross over to look at **Hammoon's church** and walk up the lane to admire the (private) **Manor Farm**.

WHAT TO LOOK FOR ⓘ

The multiple chimneys of **Fontmell Parva** (a private house) are glimpsed through the trees on this walk and there's a better view of this curious old house from the road into Child Okeford. Built of red brick and crowned with a hipped roof, it dates from 1670 and is characterised by the arched mouldings over its windows, which seem to give the house a look of surprise.

---

③ Return to the main road and turn left. After crossing the weir climb a concrete stile on the right. Head across the field bearing right, away from the treeline, to meet the river. Cross a footbridge and look left for a glimpse of the red brick **Fontmell Parva House**. Go diagonally up the field to a gateway (yellow marker) then bear right along the edge of the field, above

---

WHILE YOU'RE THERE ⓘ

On the other side of Hod Hill, the village of **Stourpaine** is worth a look. You'll have to turn down off the main road by the White Horse pub (apparently built on the side of the old, octagonal toll house) to see the best of it. Cob cottages sit snugly under thatched roofs, and a pleasing church boasts a medieval tower. The curved roof on the back of Coalport Cottage is unusual.

WHERE TO EAT AND DRINK ⓘ

The **Saxon Inn** in Child Okeford is tucked away, off the main road. It's part of a second row of houses and easy to miss if you're hurrying through the village, despite its lively sign and bright blue door. It's recommended in the *Good Beer Guide* for its ale, there's a beer garden and families are welcome.

---

the river. Go through another gateway and straight on, to a line of trees. Walk up the right side of the trees, past a chicken farm on the left.

④ Turn left at the corner of the field across a stile and go down the lane. At the road turn right into **Child Okeford** (the **Saxon Inn** is further down here, on the left). Soon turn right through a gateway and immediately go left across a stile. Walk down beside a fence, behind some houses, to cross a pair of stiles into a field. Continue along the top of this, cross another stile and go along a path behind hedges.

⑤ Emerge at a lane and turn right. Soon turn left at a stile into a field. Cross it and a second stile and follow the edge of the field round to the right. Cross a pair of stiles, go over a muddy track, cross two more stiles and bear left beside a stream. Walk along the edge of the field, cross a stile and keep straight on. Cross yet another pair of stiles then bear diagonally left across the field to reach a raised footbridge. Over this, keep straight on across a concrete bridge and bear right towards a bridge in the hedge Cross over and bear left to the corner of the field, to return to the start.

Follow Me to Fiddleford

Discover two contrasting ancient mills and an extraordinary manor house, along the banks of the River Stour.

•**DISTANCE**•	5¼ miles (8.4km)
•**MINIMUM TIME**•	3hrs
•**ASCENT / GRADIENT**•	429ft (150m) ▲▲▲
•**LEVEL OF DIFFICULTY**•	🚶🚶🚶
•**PATHS**•	Grassy paths, muddy woodland tracks, a rutted lane, roadside walking, pavements, 9 stiles
•**LANDSCAPE**•	Little hills, valleys and settlements of Blackmoor Vale
•**SUGGESTED MAP**•	aqua3 OS Explorer 129 Yeovil & Sherborne
•**START / FINISH**•	Grid reference: ST 781135
•**DOG FRIENDLINESS**•	Requested to keep on lead through first section
•**PARKING**•	Signposted Sturminster Newton Mill, off A357 just west of Old Town Bridge to south of town
•**PUBLIC TOILETS**•	At Sturminster Newton Mill, open all year

BACKGROUND TO THE WALK

Sturminster Newton consists of two separate entities linked in the 16th century by the Town Bridge. At its heart is the triangular market place, dominated by the Swan Hotel. William Barnes, a prominent Dorset dialect poet, was born near here in 1801. A newly married Thomas Hardy wrote *The Return of the Native* (1878) during the two years that he lived here, in a house overlooking Newton Mill. In Hardy's novel a despairing Eustacia Vye drowns herself in Shadwater weir. Hardy surely had in mind the thundering waters of the two mills on this walk, which dizzy the senses with their constant roar. Newton Mill, dating from the 17th century, has been restored to working order and can be seen in operation on summer weekends.

Fiddleford Mill

The tawny buildings of Fiddleford Mill, set amid pollarded willows, poplars and tall reedbeds beside the curving River Stour, create altogether quieter images reminiscent of a painting by John Constable. The Romans called this place Fitela's Ford, and the mill gets a mention in the Domesday Book of 1086. The mill building itself is tiny compared with Newton Mill. One wall is largely taken up by an inscription from 1566. It exhorts the miller to welcome all comers and to be honest in his dealings. In the 18th century a notorious smuggler called Roger Ridout hid his contraband here.

Fiddleford Manor

Fiddleford's real treasure lies on the other side of the handsome farmhouse. It is the remains of the much older and grander Fiddleford Manor, built around 1374 for William Latimer. It came into the family of Thomas White and his wife Ann, who undertook much rebuilding in the period 1539–55. Their initials appear carved into the tops of the doorways in the passage. The east wing was demolished in the 18th century in favour of a new house, itself demolished in 1956. Abandoned and derelict, the medieval remainder – with its shortened hall – was given to the state and is now in the care of English Heritage. The remarkable little building you walk into today consists of a buttery and passage beside a high-roofed, timbered hall, with stairs leading up to a solar and gallery. The roof beams once supported a flat, moulded ceiling (removed to the manor at Hinton St Mary). Now the exposed oak timbers stretch up to the apex of the roof and are revealed in all their glory. They are adorned with carved, curved wind braces that have cusps and clover-leaf holes, like the stonework of some sweeping Gothic cathedral. Viewed up close, you can see the paler timbers of restoration, inset in 1980. Recent work has revealed that the solar room was once highly painted, and you can see tantalising fragments of an angel.

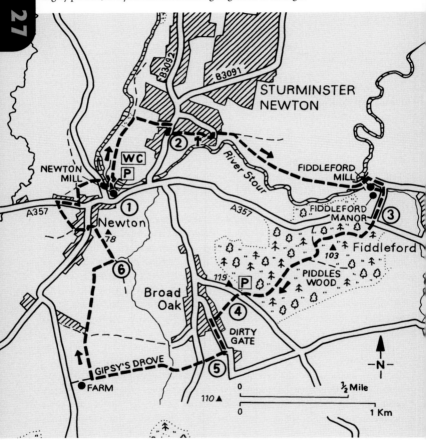

Walk 27 Directions

① Go past the **mill** and over the bridges, to the right of the pond, and through a gate into a field. Keep left up the edge, parallel with the **Stour**. Go through a gate and up an avenue of trees. Turn right along the tarmac path, then go past the playground into **Ricketts Lane**. Cross the high street and turn right.

② Turn left by the **Old Malt House**, to the church. At the end of the churchyard bear right, through the gate to go down some steps and into a lane. This bends round to the left. Take the path on the right to **Fiddleford Mill**. Go through a gate and straight on over the field, above the river. Cross a stile and bear left along a hedge. Continue straight ahead. At the far, right-hand corner cross two footbridges and the mill-race, to bear right, past the mill. Go down the drive, turn right and right again through a car park to **Fiddleford Manor**. Return to the lane and turn right.

> ### WHERE TO EAT AND DRINK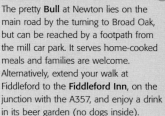
> The pretty **Bull** at Newton lies on the main road by the turning to Broad Oak, but can be reached by a footpath from the mill car park. It serves home-cooked meals and families are welcome. Alternatively, extend your walk at Fiddleford to the **Fiddleford Inn**, on the junction with the A357, and enjoy a drink in its beer garden (no dogs inside).

> ### WHAT TO LOOK FOR
> **Piddles Wood** and **Broad Oak** are part of a nature reserve, which covers some 50 acres (20ha) of semi-natural woodland. While the trees are predominantly oak and coppiced hazel, look out for the rare wild service tree (*Sorbus torminalis*) with its deeply indented leaves. In autumn look for the spiny fruit of the sweet chestnut. Peel off the hard brown shell and crunch the pale, delicately flavoured nuts.

③ At the main road turn right then cross to a bridleway, walking straight uphill into **Piddles Wood**. At the top turn right on to a track and follow it round the the hill. Descend passing two fingerposts. Go through a gate into a car park, then bear left to the road.

④ Turn right and immediately left through a farmyard, signed 'Broad Oak'. Go straight ahead through two fields into a lane. At the end turn left down the road.

⑤ At the bottom (appropriately named **Dirty Gate**) turn right down a muddy, overgrown lane – **Gipsy's Drove**. Follow this for ¾ mile (1.2km) – it's worth persevering for the views. Turn right through a gate before a farm. At the bottom go through a gate and straight over the field. Cross the stile, then go

straight on down the field edge. Soon cross a stile on to a path. Bear right along a treeline and cross two stiles to a lane.

⑥ Turn left and, once in **Newton**, turn left and soon right into **Hillcrest Close**. Where this bends right, go straight ahead down the lane. Climb the fence (by a yellow marker) and continue down the field, with a hedge to your right. Leave via a gate at the bottom, cross the **A357** and turn right. After the town sign turn left up a track, signed 'Newton Farm'. At the fingerpost cross the stile on the right and walk across the field. Cross a stile, go through the woods behind a barn, and down some steps by a fence to another stile. Bear right on the road then soon left through a gate. Cross the picnic area to return to the car park.

> ### WHILE YOU'RE THERE
> Seek out the story of dialect poet and parson **William Barnes**. He attended the little school in Penny Street. Encouraged by the Revd T H Lane Fox, he escaped to a world of books, becoming a solicitor's clerk and a schoolmaster before studying divinity. A phenomenal linguist, he taught himself many languages, including French, Welsh and Hindustani. He died in 1886, leaving his legacy of dozens of poems of gentle observation in the Dorset dialect, which he believed to be the purest form of English.

Walk 27

Walk 28

Moving Milton Abbas

Walk from a planned village into the surrounding hills and woods.

•DISTANCE•	6½ miles (10.4km)
•MINIMUM TIME•	3hrs
•ASCENT / GRADIENT•	755ft (230m) ▲▲▲
•LEVEL OF DIFFICULTY•	🚶 🚶 🚶
•PATHS•	Village high street, easy forest roads, muddy bridleways, minor road, farm tracks, 2 stiles
•LANDSCAPE•	Villages, mixed forest, rolling farmland with hidden valleys
•SUGGESTED MAP•	aqua3 OS Explorer 117 Cerne Abbas & Bere Regis
•START / FINISH•	Grid reference: ST 806018
•DOG FRIENDLINESS•	Mostly good but some road walking
•PARKING•	On main street of Milton Abbas
•PUBLIC TOILETS•	None on route

BACKGROUND TO THE WALK

Rarely do you find a village quite as symmetrical as Milton Abbas. It is the natural order of villages to grow over generations, to sprawl a little, develop secret corners and reflect different ages and tastes in their buildings. But in Milton Abbas you will find regular, whitewashed houses, identical in design, placed neatly on either side of a narrow defile. They face each other across the open street, thatched cowl facing thatched cowl. It's unnatural and slightly eerie. On closer inspection, you see that rebels have managed to sneak on a porch here, a coat of cream-coloured paint there, but nothing to seriously spoil the effect of planned perfection. No concessions were made to the two houses that were once the bakery and the forge, although the tailor's house had bow windows for extra light.

The explanation for this curiosity lies with the great house round the corner, the dream of Joseph and Caroline Damer, who bought Milton Abbey in 1752. It was on a fabulous site, first picked out by King Athelstan in AD 935, but the house left much to be desired. In 1771 the Damers decided to build something altogether grander, and more in keeping with their rising social status, to include a landscaped park by the trendiest gardener of his day, Lancelot 'Capability' Brown. One thing was getting in their way, however: the untidy township that had grown up around the abbey was spoiling the view. It would have to go.

Consequently a neat, new hamlet was built out of sight in a narrow valley, with a new church of pinkish stone. The villagers were moved, whether they liked it or not. The houses look generous, but in fact each little block was two independent family dwellings, separated by a shared central hall. There were not enough new houses to go round and overcrowding was a problem. What the villagers had to say about the near-vertical valley walls behind their shiny new homes is not recorded. The steep terraced gardens that were eventually dug out are one of the attractive features of Milton Abbas today. The Damers are buried in splendour in the abbey church. Their house, never the architectural success they had hoped for, became a school in 1954.

Nearby Winterborne Clenston is altogether more organic. It has a Tudor manor house and a medieval tithe barn covered by a steep, chequerboard roof of alternating red and black squares. The Gothic-style Church of St Nicholas dates from 1840.

Walk **28**

Winterborne Houghton

Winterborne Clenston

▲ 120

HIGHER CLENSTON COTTAGES

TITHE BARN

CLENSTON LODGE

4

OATCLOSE WOOD

3

JUBILEE TRAIL

CHARITY WOOD

Whatcombe Wood

5

▲ 220

PARK FARM

2

HILL LODGE

Milton Abbas

▲ 179

Hilton

1

HAMBRO ARMS PH

BUSINESS UNITS

6

MILTON ABBEY

▲ 182

A

▲ 130

LITTLE HEWISH COTTAGES

HEWISH CRAFT WORKSHOP

SPRING COTTAGE

142

▲ 138

B

GALLOWS CORNER

Milborne St Andrew

0   ½ Mile

0   1 Km

N

Walk 28

Walk 28 Directions

① From the church take the road up the hill. Where the pavement ends turn left through woodland. At the top turn right, into an estate road, and right again, to meet the road into the village by **Hill Lodge**.

② Cross over and go down the private road. Follow this down to the Forestry Commission signboard and bend left then right. Before the gateway turn left up the steep path, signed 'Jubilee Way'. Pass **Park Farm** on the left and descend to a track. Turn left and soon up to the right. Bear right at the top, on to a track. Where this forks, keep right to descend through **Charity Wood**. At a crossroads keep straight ahead. At the fingerpost bear right, up the bridleway.

③ Emerge at a field to follow the path down, with **Higher Clenston Cottages** ahead. At the bottom turn right through **Winterborne Clenston**. Turn left to the church. Retrace your steps to the first barn and turn left up the steep road. This becomes a track, passing below **Clenston Lodge**.

④ Continue on to a gate into **Oatclose Wood**. The path bends up to the right. Keep right at the first

fork and left at the second. Where the path divides keep left, following blue markers. Then, where the track curves right, keep left. Cross a forest track, after which the path narrows and bends right, to a field by a gate. Turn right down the edge and, at the bottom, turn left along a track.

WHERE TO EAT AND DRINK ℹ
The **Hambro Arms** is a long, low, thatched building on the high street in Milton Abbas. Originally the Dorchester Arms, it was renamed for the new estate owner, Lord Hambro, in 1852. In summer you can enjoy a scrumptious open sandwich outside on a bench at the front, in winter retreat indoors to heartier fare. Children are welcome in the dining area, dogs must stay outside.

---

⑤ At a junction turn right. After ½ mile (800m) the track climbs gently. As it curves to the right look for a path on the left, and follow this to the field corner. Turn left up a steep track. Continue up the edge of the field, to swing right at the top. Descend to the road.

WHILE YOU'RE THERE ℹ
Call in at **Hewish Craft Workshop**, in part of the old Hewish Farm buildings, to visit the workshop of wood-turner and craftsman Iain Locke. At times you may see him working a pole lathe.

---

⑥ Cross over and walk straight up the lane, passing Luccombe business units. Pass a cottage and turn right through a gateway, up a track. (Turn left here if you're following Walk 29.) Where it almost meets the road, bear diagonally left to cross a stile in the fence. Bear left over a second stile and enter the woods. There's no clear path – keep downhill and bear left to emerge on the village street above the **school**. Turn left to return to your car.

WHAT TO LOOK FOR ℹ
Brown tourist signs point the way to **Milton Abbey**, ½ mile (800m) up the valley. The house is now a school, but you can park amid the school buildings (donation box) and walk through to the abbey church. It was rebuilt in stone and flint after a disastrous fire of 1309 and has been restored several times since. Approach from the village of Hilton for the best views.

Gallows Corner

Take a shorter walk, or extend Walk 28, to a sinister landmark.
See map and information panel for Walk 28

•DISTANCE•	5 miles (8km)
•MINIMUM TIME•	2hrs 30min
•ASCENT / GRADIENT•	663ft (202m) ▲▲▲
•LEVEL OF DIFFICULTY•	🚶🚶 🚶

Walk 29 Directions (Walk 28 option)

You can get a different view of Milton Abbas on this shorter walk, which can also be used to extend Walk 28. Take the footpath just above the church, which leads up irregular steps and a steep bank through the woods. Cross a stile at the top then go straight on, over a second stile. The path leads straight ahead across a field, over the top of a hill. Descend to a hedge. Turn left and walk along it to a farm track. Turn right and follow this down to pass a cottage on the left (if you're extending Walk 28, you join here). Go through a gateway, turn left and immediately right, down a farm lane between hedges. This leads into a field. Keep straight ahead, with a hedge on your right. Cross a stile by a gate and keep straight on, with the hedge on your left.

Cross a pair of stiles (Point Ⓐ) and turn right, up the edge of the field. Climb up to meet a green track, then continue past a dairy on to the road. Follow this to the bottom of the hill, with views to Milton Abbey on your right. Turn right along the road past **Little Hewish Cottages**. Now go left through a gate and

straight uphill (with blue bridleway markers). Officially the public bridleway goes through a gate and left, following right round the contour of the hill. However, a simpler route (recommended by the landowner) leads straight up over the top of the hill and down the other side. Either way, reach a field gate, then cross the road, go through a gate and bear diagonally right up the field. Go through a gate in the top corner, cross a strip of woodland, and pass through another gate. Go straight ahead up two fields and turn right down a green lane.

Reach the convergence of ancient routes at the high point of **Gallows Corner** (Point Ⓑ) – an eerie landmark for wayfarers. Take the track on your immediate right, which leads down through a tunnel of trees. Turn right on to the road by **Spring Cottage**. Opposite an old farmhouse hook left on the signed bridleway. Follow this track as it curves up the hill and through several fields, dipping and rising. Go through a gate and pass between some stable buildings to a road. Turn right and go down to a junction. Bear left, passing the scenic lake and the turning to the **abbey** and school. Continue up the high street to return to the church.

Hardy's Work at Turnworth

From chalky heights to visit a legacy of Thomas Hardy's early life.

•DISTANCE•	4½ miles (7.2km)
•MINIMUM TIME•	2hrs 30min
•ASCENT / GRADIENT•	155ft (59m) ▲▲▲
•LEVEL OF DIFFICULTY•	🚶 🚶 🚶
•PATHS•	Flinty tracks, bridleways, forest paths, village road, 2 stiles
•LANDSCAPE•	Farmed valleys, expansive views, windswept chalk ridge
•SUGGESTED MAP•	aqua3 OS Explorer 117 Cerne Abbas & Bere Regis
•START / FINISH•	Grid reference: ST 812093
•DOG FRIENDLINESS•	Beware of horses
•PARKING•	Car park and picnic area (very narrow entrance) just west of road, at top of hill north of Turnworth; more accessible lay-by further on, on opposite side
•PUBLIC TOILETS•	None on route

Walk 30 Directions

Thomas Hardy is well known to history as a novelist and poet, yet in his first chosen career, as an architect, he is barely a footnote.

From the picnic area go back to the road and turn right, down the hill. After a few paces turn left down a wide track, signposted as a bridleway. After a short distance, just before a wood, a narrower track is indicated off to the right. Follow this down the edge of the wood. You're on a route that will take you in a straight line down the valley for about 1½ miles (2.4km).

After about ¼ mile (400m), at the end of the wood, bear right through a gate and immediately left along a broad green ride, with a windswept hedge on your left. Go straight on through a gate (blue marker) and follow the track as it runs along the belt of woodland that borders the conifers of **Bonsley Common**.

The path descends gently, bending slightly right at the end of the woods. Stay on the track through open farmland and between hedges for ¼ mile (400m). Look out for **Shepherd's Corner Farm** down to the left, complete with a big walled garden. At a crossroads of tracks turn right. This leads steeply downhill, passing a barn on the right. At the bottom turn right and walk along the road into **Turnworth** village. The **Church of St Mary's** is one of the first buildings you see, its low grey tower peeping over the top of the vicarage

---

WHILE YOU'RE THERE

Beacons lit up the skies along the line of the Wessex Ridgeway to warn of the Spanish Armada in 1588, notably on Melbury Hill. The event was commemorated with a line of fires in July 1988, when the great beacon was raised on Okeford Hill. You may have to climb the gate to reach it, but there is a bridleway here giving public access to the gaunt iron basket. The view is, of course, superb.

on the left. The carved stone foliage for the church's pillars were designed by Thomas Hardy (although the work was done later).

Thomas Hardy was born into a family of builders and stonemasons, so it was natural enough that at the age of 16 he should start architectural studies with John Hicks of Dorchester. In 1862 he moved to London, where he specialised in church restoration work for Arthur Blomfield. Returning to Dorset five years later, Hardy continued to undertake intermittent architectural work. His most visible achievement in this field is his own house at Max Gate, Dorchester, which he started in 1885, but it's hardly a masterpiece.

> ### WHERE TO EAT AND DRINK ℹ
> On the main street of Okeford Fitzpaine, just off the square, you'll find the old red brick **Royal Oak**. It's open lunchtimes and evenings for jacket potatoes, grills, curries and home-made steak and kidney pie. Dogs are welcome in the bar with its massive beamed inglenook fireplace. Children are welcome in the lounge bar.

Pass the **Old Post Office** (now a B&B) on the right and take the track up to the left. Just after a cottage turn up to the right by a yellow marker, heading diagonally left up the field. At the top corner go through a gateway and keep in a straight line, bearing diagonally left across the field through a gap under a large ash tree. Continue on this line, bearing right across the corner of the field under a great oak tree, to reach a stile in a fence. Cross this and bear diagonally left down the steep hill. Below, on the right, you will see **Turnworth House**, not very grand despite its attractive park setting and huge walled garden.

> ### WHAT TO LOOK FOR ℹ
> In **St Mary's Church** at Turnworth look for an unusual memorial stone in the north aisle, inscribed with barely decipherable Latin text. The translation tells that John Straight, a 17th-century vicar, was determined to have a memorial to himself created during his lifetime, to record his success in reclaiming massive back-taxes for the church. Look out for the the carved owl corbel below the tower. Straight was also vicar at Stourpaine (► Walk 26), where there's a kneeling effigy of him.

Cross a track and keep going down, to reach a gate behind a barn (yellow marker). Go through it and walk round to a road. Turn left, with **Okeden House** ahead.

Opposite the house go through a gate on the right and head up the steep road. Tarmac soon gives way to track. Go through the gate and continue straight on. The track curls left round the top of the woods. Look for a marker on the fence post and bear diagonally right, up the flinty field, passing close to stacks of seasoning timber. Bear left along the tree line towards the top of the hill. Where the track swings sharply left, look for a yellow marker on a small wooden gate on your right. Go through this and turn left up the edge of the field. The ridges and ditches to your right are signs of ancient settlement – this is **Ringmoor** (owned by the National Trust). Pass the ruins of a farm on the left and reach a gate. Go through this, pass a pond and go through another gate. Turn right on to the **Wessex Ridgeway** path and follow this for ¾ mile (1.2km), gently downhill with outstanding views to the north west. Just before the road turn left over a stile to re-enter the picnic area.

Walk 31

Living on the Edge at Ibberton

From the tops of Bulbarrow Hill to the valley floor and back, via an atmospheric church.

•DISTANCE•	4¼ miles (6.8km)
•MINIMUM TIME•	2hrs
•ASCENT / GRADIENT•	591ft (180m) ▲▲▲
•LEVEL OF DIFFICULTY•	🚶 🚶 🚶
•PATHS•	Quiet roads, muddy bridleways, field paths, 2 stiles
•LANDSCAPE•	Edge of steep escarpment with views over Blackmoor Vale
•SUGGESTED MAP•	aqua3 OS Explorer 117 Cerne Abbas & Bere Regis
•START / FINISH•	Grid reference: ST 791071
•DOG FRIENDLINESS•	Lots of road walking may be tiring for soft paws
•PARKING•	Car park at Ibberton Hill picnic site
•PUBLIC TOILETS•	None on route

BACKGROUND TO THE WALK

The Wessex Ridgeway is a long distance footpath that runs for 137 miles (220km) from Marlborough in Wiltshire across Dorset to the coastal town of Lyme Regis. The 62 miles (100km) of the Dorset section start at the high point of Ashmore (► Walk 21). Although it was only completed in 1980, it follows, as far as possible, much older routes across the hills and downs. It is frequently criss-crossed by the routes in this book. This walk uses a good stretch of it, on the chalk ridge between Okeford Hill and Bulbarrow Hill.

Ridgeway Panorama

The view from the Ridgeway at this point is captivating. You're 902 feet (275m) above sea level and from the viewing table you can identify the distant Blackdown and Quantock hills to the left, the symmetrical mound of Glastonbury Tor ahead, and, to your right, Shaftesbury and Cranborne Chase. Immediately below, beyond the steep bank of golden-flowered gorse, the patchwork fields of the Blackmoor Vale are spread out in all shades of green and brown, textured with clumps of trees and widely scattered dwellings and farms. Even today they are the little communities, linked by a network of hedges and lanes, which Thomas Hardy captured so well in his novels and poetry.

Elusive St Eustace

Tucked under the hill and spreading up its flank, Ibberton is a particular delight, a blend of stone, flint and thatch and old and new houses side by side. When I walked through the village some local people urged me to visit their church, describing it as somewhere very special. One of only three in the country dedicated to St Eustace, it sits high above the village. The church is reached by a steep, rocky path and has an enviable view over the valley. Its grey stone is silvered with lichen and the wall by the door leans alarmingly. Inside there is a tranquil atmosphere of light and space. Fragments of medieval glass splash gold in the otherwise plain leaded windows. There are no pews, but wooden chairs are ranged around, giving the feel that this is a well-used community space. Faded photographs show the church in a state of collapse during rebuilding in 1901, with its entire end wall down. There was also a wooden gallery still in existence around that time. A hollowed out millstone was once the only font.

The memorial to a young man killed in the First World War is on a touchingly human scale too, with a tiny painted portrait hanging on a pillar. He was Charles Hugh Plowman, the rector's younger son. He died in far-off Macedonia, leaving no mortal remains to be returned to his grieving family. With three other villagers, he is also remembered on the war memorial – the church clock. The villagers are right – it's a remarkable place.

Walk 31

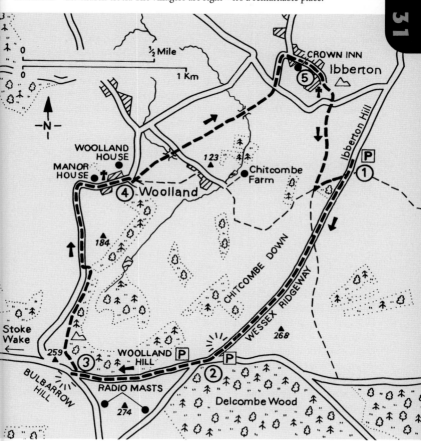

① Turn left along the road, following the route of the **Wessex Ridgeway**, with the village of Ibberton below you to the right. The road climbs gradually, with the masts on **Bulbarrow Hill** ahead.

② After a mile (1.6km) pass a car park on the left, with a viewing table. At a junction bear right and immediately right again, signposted 'Stoke Wake'. Pass another car park on the right. The woods of **Woolland Hill** now fall away steeply on your right. Pass the radio masts to your left and reach a small gate

Walk 31

into a field on your right, near the end of the wood. Before taking it, go the extra few steps to the road junction ahead for a wonderful view of the escarpment stretching away to the west.

③ Go through the gate and follow the uneven bridleway down. Glimpse a spring-fed lake through the trees on the right. At the bottom the path swings left to a gate. Go through this, on to a road. Turn right, continuing downhill with a rich variety of plant life at eye-level. Follow the road into Woolland, passing the **Manor House** and the **Old Schoolhouse**, on your left and right respectively.

WHERE TO EAT AND DRINK ℹ

The 16th-century **Crown Inn** at Ibberton has a magnificent flagstone floor inside and sunny beer gardens outside. Its ancient, studded oak door opens to the tantalising smell of good food. Dogs are not allowed inside, but children are welcome under proper supervision.

---

④ Just beyond the entrance to **Woolland House** turn right into a lane and immediately left through a kissing gate. The path immediately forks. Take the left-hand track, down through some marshy patches and a stand of young sycamores. Posts with yellow footpath waymarkers lead straight on across

---

WHAT TO LOOK FOR ℹ

The waymarker for the Wessex Ridgeway is a green and white disc showing a two-legged, winged dragon called a **wyvern**, which is a symbol associated with the ancient kingdom of Wessex. The path reflects the route of an ancient, much longer highway called the Great Ridgeway that was once used to transport goods between Devon and the North Norfolk coast.

WHILE YOU'RE THERE ℹ

Explore Ibberton more thoroughly by picking up a leaflet for the village's **Millennium Path** – you'll find them freely available in the pub and the church. The 2¼ mile (3.6km) pink-waymarked route takes you around the back lanes between the cottages. Stiles have been replaced by gates to make the going easier.

---

the meadow, with gorse-clad **Chitcombe Down** up to the right. Cross a footbridge over the stream. Go straight on to cross a road. Keeping straight on, go through a kissing gate in the hedge. Bear left down the field, cross a stile and continue down. Cross a footbridge and stile to bear left across the next field. Go through a gate to a road junction. Walk straight up the road ahead and follow it right, into **Ibberton**. Bear right to reach the **Crown Inn**.

⑤ Continue up this road through the village. The path becomes very steep. There are some steps that lead up to the church. Continue up the steep path. Cross the road and go straight ahead through the gate. Keep straight on along a fence, climbing steadily. Cross under some power lines and bear left up the next field, to a small gate in the hedge. Turn left up the field edge, then go through the gate at the top on to the road, finally turning left to return to the car park.

A Lost Village at Higher Melcombe

A hilly circuit of farmland where, in centuries past, labour economics determined the pattern of settlement.

•DISTANCE•	5 miles (8km)
•MINIMUM TIME•	2hrs 30min
•ASCENT / GRADIENT•	443ft (135m) ▲▲▲
•LEVEL OF DIFFICULTY•	🚶🚶 🚶🚶 🚶
•PATHS•	Farmland, woodland track, ancient bridleway, road, 13 stiles
•LANDSCAPE•	Gently rolling farmland, little lumpy hills, village
•SUGGESTED MAP•	aqua3 OS Explorer 117 Cerne Abbas & Bere Regis
•START / FINISH•	Grid reference: ST 765031
•DOG FRIENDLINESS•	Some road walking, one unfriendly stile
•PARKING•	Small parking area on north side of village hall
•PUBLIC TOILETS•	None on route

BACKGROUND TO THE WALK

Be prepared for confusion on this walk: it passes Higher Melcombe and through Melcombe Bingham to Bingham's Melcombe, which is also known as Melcombe Horsey. And Melcombe Horsey was the name of a village at Higher Melcombe that has now disappeared. Is that clear?

There has been a church at Bingham's Melcombe since before 1302. The current one dates from the 14th century. The roving bell, *Regina Coeli Alla Alla*, was sold twice to raise funds for the church but kept coming back, eventually resting on the floor for 50 years until the money could be raised to rehang it. Today it's safely back with its companion *O Beata Trinitas* in the belfry, although only chiming is allowed.

The Binghams

The church is cruciform in shape, two side chapels forming the arms of the cross. The Bingham chapel has a touching memorial to Thomas, infant son of Richard and Philadelphia Bingham, who died in 1711. The Binghams were one of Dorset's leading Parliamentary families during the Civil War, and their mansion and gardens (not open to the public), of which you can only catch a glimpse, are magnificent. The Dower House, opposite the church, has fine octagonal window panes.

By contrast, Higher Melcombe is, today, a solitary farm, set in a fertile green basin at the head of a valley. The buildings are dominated by the old manor house, built in the mid-15th century for Sir John Horsey, with a chapel attached later. A village called Melcombe Horsey once occupied this lovely spot. According to the map the village simply disappeared in medieval times, but why? Unlike Milton Abbas (➤ Walk 28) there is no sign of grand rebuilding necessitating removal.

What could cause rural depopulation on such a scale? The answer lies at Dorset's other Melcombe, the port of Melcombe Regis, now absorbed into the sprawl of Weymouth. Melcombe Regis has an unfortunate claim to fame for, in June 1348, the first case in Britain of bubonic plague – the Black Death – was brought ashore here. The disease, carried by fleas that were equally at home on black rats or people, spread through the county with devastating speed, wiping out between one third and one half of the population.

Feudal Inefficiencies

The feudal system that had operated until this time in Dorset, in which labourers had been tied to manorial land, could not survive in the face of such losses. With a drastic shortage of able bodies, labour became a prime commodity. Workers simply moved to where they could be paid for their work as free men. Once-thriving villages, such as Melcombe Horsey were reduced to little hamlets, or sometimes just a single, isolated farm. The changes meant a great reduction in arable cultivation, to the extent that some prime farmland reverted to more manageable grazing.

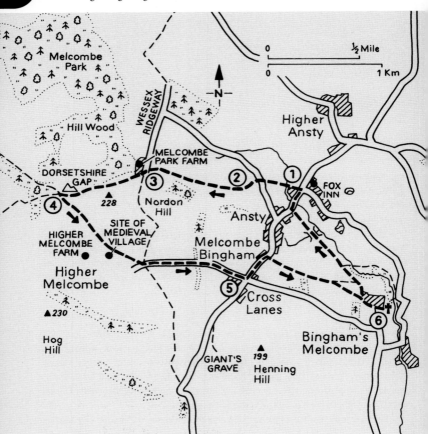

Walk 32 Directions

① Turn up the road and go immediately left down a waymarked path. Cross a stile,

bear right down the edge of the field and cross a stile at the bottom. Continue straight up the next field, cross a stile and road to go through a gate. Keep straight on to reach a pair of stiles in a hedge.

② Go through these stiles then bear right, across the field. Descend and go right, through a gate in the corner. Follow the track beside a hedge, then go through a gate and bend to the left.

WHAT TO LOOK FOR ⓘ

Ansty's handsome, flint and brick village hall is called the **Old Brewery Hall**. It was the original brewery for Hall and Woodhouse beer, made since 1777. The brewery's early success was founded on a government contract to supply ale to Dorsetshire troops awaiting an invasion by Napoleon that never came. Hall and Woodhouse moved to Blandford St Mary in 1899 and still thrive there today under their better-known Badger trademark.

---

③ Go into the farm and turn immediately left through the furthest of three gates, signposted '**Wessex Ridgeway**'. Walk along the edge of the field, above a wood. Go through a gate and continue straight ahead along the top of the ridge, enjoying superb views over the Blackmoor Vale. The track descends abruptly. Turn right, through a gate, to a crossroads of tracks at the **Dorsetshire Gap**.

④ Turn left down a bridleway through a deep cleft, signposted 'Higher Melcombe'. Keep straight

---

WHILE YOU'RE THERE ⓘ

Why should the understanding of lumps and bumps in the landscape be left to dry archaeology? And what better explanation for a burial mound some 23ft (7m) long than that a giant lies entombed there? Take the footpath up the western slope of Henning Hill, to the south of Melcombe Bingham. A terrace on the hillside is where you'll find the **Giant's Grave**. A so-called pillow mound lies near by, and there are good views along the valley.

---

on through three fields. Ridges and hummocks in a field to your right are the only sign of the medieval village. Pass **Higher Melcombe** farm, then go through a gate and turn left, on to a minor road. Bear right to walk down an avenue of young trees (look right to see the hill track leading to the Giant's Grave). Descend past some houses to a junction.

⑤ Turn left and walk on the road into **Melcombe Bingham**. Pass a row of houses then turn right. Go through a gate to take the path straight ahead across the field. Pass the end of a strip of woodland and maintain your direction up the fence towards a hut. Cross the fence at the top. Continue ahead, down the field towards **Bingham's Melcombe**. Cross a stile and turn right. Follow the drive round and down to the church.

WHERE TO EAT AND DRINK ⓘ

The **Fox Inn** at Ansty bills itself as 'The Country Retreat'. Inside the wood panelling gleams. You can get morning coffees, afternoon teas and snacks at the bar (where dogs are welcome) or treat yourself to a meal in one of the two restaurants. Children are welcome throughout the pub.

---

⑥ Retrace your route to the stile and keep straight on past, up the field. Before the end turn left through a gate and bear right along a path. Where this divides keep left. Go through a gate and descend on a track. Go straight ahead to cross a footbridge. Keep straight on, bear right over a stile in the fence and continue down the field. When under some bulging trees turn left over a stile. Keep straight ahead then cross a stile on to the road. Turn right to return to your car.

The Dairies of Marnhull

On the level through pastures that owe their presence to mechanised farming.

•DISTANCE•	4 miles (6.4km)
•MINIMUM TIME•	2hrs 30min
•ASCENT / GRADIENT•	115ft (35m) ▲ ▲ ▲
•LEVEL OF DIFFICULTY•	👫 👫 👫
•PATHS•	Village roads, pasture (wellies advised in winter), 14 stiles
•LANDSCAPE•	Green vale, surrounded by low hills
•SUGGESTED MAP•	aqua3 OS Explorer 129 Yeovil & Sherborne
•START / FINISH•	Grid reference: ST 774193
•DOG FRIENDLINESS•	Beware of electric fences in fields; control needed through farmyards and care across high bridges
•PARKING•	Small car park (free) in Marnhull village, opposite butcher
•PUBLIC TOILETS•	None on route

BACKGROUND TO THE WALK

In winter the fields of the broad Blackmoor Vale gleam and glint with standing water. The dampness and the soft, sweet air make for lush green meadows and, where there's rich pasture like this, there are dairy cattle. In the Blackmoor Vale, there are thousands of them, mainly black and white Holstein-Friesians. In spring and summer they graze their way slowly through the fields on a regular routine. In late autumn, when the ground becomes too churned up by their hoofs, they are herded into vast byres, from where they stare out balefully at passing walkers, through clouds of steamy breath, waiting for a warm, dry day when they, too, will be free to kick up their heels.

Money in the Slurry

Any doubts that dairying is big business are soon dispelled in this part of Dorset, where a strong whiff of slurry often taints the wind. As you gaze around the big-eyed, chomping herds, you can believe that UK dairy farms produce around 3.15 billion gallons (14.3 billion litres) of milk a year, part of a total market for milk, cream, cheese, butter and yoghurt that stands at some £6 billion.

Until the development of refrigeration and pasteurisation, milk was a highly perishable commodity. Dairy herds were kept on the fringes of towns to minimise the delay between milking and getting the milk to the consumer, by hand or cart. Furthermore, prior to mechanisation, milking was a laborious, manual job and the risk of bacterial infection and contamination was much higher. Tess's experiences as a milkmaid in Hardy's *Tess of the D'Urbervilles* (1861) give a good picture of this way of rural life. The little old barns of the third farm on this walk, Gomershay, are a poignant reminder.

Everything changed with the advent of mass refrigeration, to slow the bacteria, and pasteurisation to kill them off. The cows are milked by vacuum suction pumps on the farm, and efficiency is such that one cow can produce up to 1,320 gallons (6,000 litres) of milk in a year. Refrigerated road tankers transfer it to a central dairy where it is checked for bacteria before being pasteurised, processed and sent out, with an extended shop shelf-life. There are downsides to the success story, as with any industrial production or intensive farming, not least of which are concerns about livestock welfare. High levels of fertiliser and overflowing slurry pits contribute to around a quarter of water pollution incidents. Ruminating cattle produce vast amounts of methane gas, adding steadily to the perceived problems of global warming. Yet it is estimated that we drink around four times as much of the white stuff as our predecessors and, while the market continues to reinvent itself (who bought semi-skimmed 20 years ago?), there seems little likelihood of it slowing down.

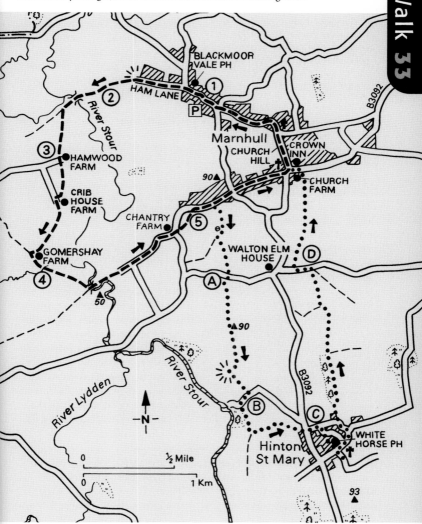

Walk 33 Directions

① Turn left out of the car park and walk along **Burton Street**, passing a row of shops. Pass the **Blackmoor**

Vale pub and keep straight on, down **Ham Lane**. At the end there is a superb view over the valley and Henstridge. Follow the footpath sign straight ahead down the field, with trees on the left.

Walk 33

② At the bottom of the field the track curves left and disappears – turn right here to walk down the field edge. Cross a stile and bear left to cross the footbridge over the **River Stour**. Continue straight ahead. Cross a stile in the hedge, then a footbridge and another stile, and bear left across the field towards **Hamwood Farm**.

③ Keep to the right of the biggest barn, to pass through the farmyard with the farmhouse to your right-hand side. Cross a lane, go through a gate and head diagonally right towards a stile, passing close to a telegraph pole. Cross a bridge and head right, across the field, towards **Crib House Farm**. Cross over a pair of stiles then go left, around the field edge. Climb the stile in the corner and turn left down the road.

Just before a farmyard turn right, through the first gate. Now bear right across the field. Cross another bridge and make for **Gomershay Farm**. Turn right past the first byre and then turn left and right through the farmyard. At the other side of the barns turn left and pass the farmhouse itself. Continue up a lane, passing a small barn. By an old truck bear right over the brow of the field, then cross a bridge over a meander of the river.

④ At the other side of the footbridge keep to the right, past the curve of the stream, and head straight up through a gate. Walk up the next field and cross a stile on to the lane. Follow this up to a junction by **Chantry Farm**. Cross the road and go into the field. Head diagonally left, cross a stile in the bottom corner, and walk along the edge of the next field.

⑤ Cross a stile into the road and turn right back in to Marnhull village. (Turn right here for the extra loop of Walk 34.) Go past the school to the parish church. Turn left down **Church Hill** (Walk 34 rejoins the route here). Follow this road as it winds through the village, eventually becoming **Burton Street** by the Methodist church. Walk past the post office and return to the car park at the start.

Pursuing Tess

An extra loop follows Tess's flight to Hinton St Mary.
See map and information panel for Walk 33

•DISTANCE•	7½ miles (12.1km)
•MINIMUM TIME•	4hrs
•ASCENT / GRADIENT•	229ft (70m) ▲ ▲ ▲
•LEVEL OF DIFFICULTY•	🚶 🚶 🚶

Walk 34 Directions
(Walk 33 option)

After Point ⑤ on Walk 33, take the first lane right and go down the private road. Pass **Goddard's Farm**, go round a pond then through a gate and bear left, up the field edge. Soon go though a pair of gates and bear right. Cross a stile and pass a tree line to cross another. Continue with **Walton Elm House** on the left.

Bearing right, go over a stile into **Mowes Lane**, Point Ⓐ. Go up the drive ahead and keep left by the hedge. At the far corner cross a stile into a copse. Cross another stile and keep straight on by the fence. Cross a pair of stiles and bear right, round the field. Bear right through a gap and continue along the trees. Cross a stile into a lane and turn right.

Near the bottom turn left on a bridleway through a gate, Point Ⓑ. Bear left, then right up a wide green ride, above woods. Keep ahead through a gateway and turn left up the field edge. Before the end turn right, cross a stile and bear left. Cross two stiles and head right, towards **Hinton St Mary**. Go through a gate and bear left, by a garage, to the road, Point Ⓒ.

Cross and go up the lane opposite. Take the first road on the right. Where this sweeps left go straight ahead, into a field. Go through a gate at the far side into a back lane, passing the **Village Garden** on the right. Cross the road and take the raised pavement to the churchyard. Retrace your steps, turn right opposite the **White Horse**, and walk through the village. The road curls down to the left. Turn left at the junction – the road narrows by **Mead Cottage**. Where it swings left, bear right through a gateway. Now head down the hill, aiming for **St Gregory's Church** in Marnhull. Follow the track through some woods. At the end bear right over the field, cross a footbridge and bear right, uphill. Cross a track then go over a footbridge and stile. Continue up the field to a road, Point Ⓓ.

Turn left then take the footpath on the right, climbing the gate into the field. Go straight over, climb another gate and bear right. Cross a footbridge and keep left. Then turn left, over a stile. Walk up to the farm. Bear right to a gate in the top corner. Go through and turn left through **Church Farm** to the road. Cross and turn left, passing the **Crown Inn**. Turn right down **Church Hill**, rejoining Walk 33.

Walk 35

Hitting the Deck at Henstridge

Walk across the Blackmoor Vale, where wartime pilots learnt their skills.

•DISTANCE•	4½ miles (7.2km)
•MINIMUM TIME•	3hrs
•ASCENT / GRADIENT•	262ft (80m)
•LEVEL OF DIFFICULTY•	
•PATHS•	Lanes, grassy, muddy farmland, 8 stiles, 3 gates to climb
•LANDSCAPE•	Hillside village and pastoral farmland
•SUGGESTED MAP•	aqua3 OS Explorer 129 Yeovil & Sherborne
•START / FINISH•	Grid reference: ST 768231
•DOG FRIENDLINESS•	Lead essential through farmyards; some lifting over stiles
•PARKING•	Lay-by above church, Church Lane, Kington Magna
•PUBLIC TOILETS•	None on route

Walk 35 Directions

Walk down the hill and take the second entrance, up some steps, into the churchyard. **Kington Magna's pond** lies just below. The village looks out over the Blackmoor Vale to Henstridge, on the Somerset border.

Henstridge Airfield was on the valley floor over to the left. During the Second World War this huge airfield was built for training Fleet Air Arm (Royal Navy) pilots. Named HMS *Dipper* and commissioned in 1943, it covered 355 acres (144ha) and was provided

with five runways. A distinctive feature was the 'dummy deck' runway, for learning how to land on aircraft carriers. For 3½ years the skies were filled with Fairey Fulmars and Barracudas, Supermarine Spitfires and Seafires and other aircraft, before the site was closed. Pitted fragments of the runways survive – they're mostly used for storing new cars, but one section continues as a private airfield.

Walk past the **church** and leave the churchyard via a wooden gate, heading down a grassy path through the field. Keep straight down and, at the bottom corner, go through a kissing gate into a road by **Gilly Flower Cottage**.

Bear right and the road soon narrows into a back lane. Reach a road and turn right. Where the road swings right keep straight ahead then turn sharp left at the fence, to walk along a gravel path. Go through a gate into a playing field and straight on through the kissing

WHILE YOU'RE THERE

Nip over the border into Somerset and visit **Henstridge Airfield**, home of the bright yellow Dorset Air Ambulance, to watch the light aircraft buzzing in and out. Old photos on the walls recall its wartime heyday, and you can get a cup of tea and a snack while you soak up the relaxed atmosphere at the control centre.

gate opposite. Turn right and follow the fence round, to pass through another kissing gate by a bungalow. A short track leads you to a road, **Back Lane**. Turn left and follow this down, passing the **Old Rectory** on your left. Cross the lane at the end and go through a gate. Bear slightly left across the field towards another gate. Go through this and turn left across the top corner, towards a stile in the hedgerow. Cross a pair of stiles and a footbridge, and head straight across the field towards the corner of a hedge. Go through a gate and turn right down the lane. At **Lower Farm** turn left into a muddy field. Walk straight ahead and go through two gates to a road. Immediately turn right into a rutted green lane between hedges. Cross a stile at the end and head straight on, diagonally across the field, towards a gateway. Pass through and bear slightly right across the next field. Keep to the right of a tree and pass the end of a hedge to a gate.

WHERE TO EAT AND DRINK ℹ️

The **Ship Inn** on the A30 at nearby West Stour is well worth the detour, not only for its food but also for its heritage. On the old summer coaching route from London to Exeter, it has stories of highway robbery and a chamber with barred windows used by the dreaded press gang. Dogs and children welcome.

Go through this and cross the **A30** with care. Walk straight on, up **Coking Lane**. Go straight ahead through the farmyard and bear slightly right on the other side, crossing a sleeper footbridge to walk up the side of the hedge. Follow the hedge to the end and, where the field narrows, bear diagonally left to go through an overgrown gate in the corner. A few

paces on, the next gate has collapsed – clamber over and keep ahead up the edge of the field. Turn left along the top of the field and go through a gate. Continue straight on and go through another gate. Turn right and follow the field edge. Just before the road there's a gap where you can get through on to the road (if it's impassable, keep round the field boundary to a gate).

Turn left and walk along the road towards **Fifehead Magdalen**. Opposite **My Lady's Cottage** go left through a squeeze gate in the hedge. Walk straight across the field, passing through a gap into a second field. Cross the stile into **Fifehead Wood**. Keep straight ahead on the broad path and cross a stile at the other side, by a gate.

Head diagonally left up the field to cross a stile in the hedge. Look left to see what's left of the airstrip at Henstridge pointing towards you. Continue towards the top left corner of the next field. In the corner cross the bridge and emerge on to the **A30**. Turn left for a couple of paces and cross over with care, going straight through the hedge to cross another bridge and stile into a field. Head slightly left across the field. Cross a footbridge and stile in the corner into another field. Keep left, go through a gate, then directly through the farmyard and down the straight farm road. At the end turn right up **Chapel Hill**, passing the Primitive Methodist chapel of 1851. Turn left just after **Horse Shoe Cottage** and follow the road to **Gilly Flower Cottage**. Turn right through the kissing gate and retrace your steps up to the church. Pass an ancient yew then leave the churchyard via the top gate to return to your car.

By Hardy's Cottage and 'Egdon Heath'

A circuit across wooded heath and farmland to the place where Hardy, quite literally, left his heart.

•DISTANCE•	5 miles (8km)
•MINIMUM TIME•	2hrs
•ASCENT / GRADIENT•	328ft (100m) ▲▲▲
•LEVEL OF DIFFICULTY•	🚶🚶 🚶🚶 🚶🚶
•PATHS•	Woodland and heathland tracks, muddy field paths and bridleways, firm paths, road, 15 stiles
•LANDSCAPE•	Woodland, tree-clad heath, open meadows, waterway, rolling farmland
•SUGGESTED MAP•	aqua3 OS Explorer 117 Cerne Abbas & Bere Regis
•START / FINISH•	Grid reference: SY 725921
•DOG FRIENDLINESS•	Not allowed in Hardy's garden or cottage; deer shooting year-round in woods – keep dogs close
•PARKING•	Thorncombe Wood (donations) below Hardy's Cottage
•PUBLIC TOILETS•	None on route; nearest north west on A35

BACKGROUND TO THE WALK

You can't go far in Dorset without coming across references to novelist and poet Thomas Hardy (1840–1928). Writing about a rural scene that was already vanishing at the end of the 19th century, he did more than anybody to establish an identity for the county, which he thinly disguised as a fictional Wessex. His complicated tales of thwarted desire and human failing, littered with memorable, realistic characters and evocative descriptions of recognisable places, have become literary classics.

Hardy was born at Higher Bockhampton in the cottage built by his great grandfather, set in a lovely garden. The cottage is now owned by the National Trust, however a much better collection of Hardy relics is held in Dorchester's museum, which includes a re-creation of his study. Hardy went to school locally and later in Dorchester. He joined his father playing fiddle in the lively Stinsford church band. Apprenticed as an architect, he befriended the dialect poet William Barnes (▶ Walk 27), but it was several years before his own poetry started to appear in print.

Retreat to Dorset

In 1867 he retired to Dorset for health reasons and began writing seriously. His first published novel was *Desperate Remedies* (1871), swiftly followed by *Under the Greenwood Tree* (1872), *A Pair of Blue Eyes* (1873) and *Far From the Madding Crowd* (1874). Riding on the success of this last book he married Emma Gifford and they lived for a time at Sturminster Newton (▶ Walk 27). Success followed success, and the highlights of this profitable period include *The Return of the Native* (1878), *The Mayor of Casterbridge* (1886), *The Woodlanders* (1887, Hardy's own declared favourite), *Tess of the D'Urbervilles* (1891) and *Jude the Obscure* (1895).

Walk 36

National Treasure

In 1885 Hardy and his wife moved to the home he had designed at Max Gate, on the outskirts of Dorchester (his Casterbridge), and he remained there for the rest of his life. Emma died, estranged and childless, in 1912, and two years later Thomas married Florence Dugdale. In 1928, when he died, Hardy was a celebrated grand old man of letters, in fact, a national treasure. He was buried in Westminster Abbey. He had requested that his heart, however, be buried in Stinsford (his Mellstock) churchyard, and so, unusually, he has two graves, the latter lying between the tombs of his two wives.

The Hardy influence is still strong in Dorset. Fact and fiction become blurred in 'Tess's Cottage', and many pubs proudly identify themselves as their fictional counterpart. A long distance footpath, the Hardy Way, links many of his favourite sites.

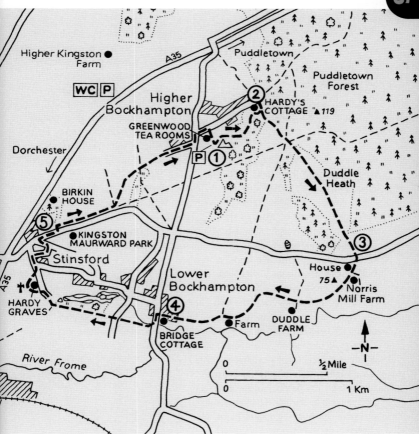

Walk 36 **Directions**

① Take the steep woodland path to the right of the display boards, signposted 'Hardy's Cottage'. Turn left at the fingerpost and follow the

winding route down to a crossroads of tracks, marked by a monument. Turn left for **Hardy's Cottage**.

② Retrace your route up behind the cottage and bear left, signed 'Rushy Pond'. At a crossroads take the path signed 'Norris Mill'. Where the path forks bear right. Cross a track then head down between rhododendrons. Emerge on to heathland and stay on the path. Follow markers down to the right. Descend, cross a stile and bear right. Cross a pair of stiles and turn left up the field, towards a house.

WHILE YOU'RE THERE i

Visit the formal Edwardian gardens and extensive parkland of **Kingston Maurwood**. They include a rose garden, a Japanese garden, an outstanding double herbaceous border and an unusual red garden. The Georgian house is now occupied by an agricultural college. There's also a lively farm animal park (including llamas) for children to enjoy and a visitor centre.

---

③ Cross the road on to a farm track. Bear right before some barns, cross a stile and continue up the track. After a gate bear right over a field. Cross a pair of stiles in the hedge, then go straight ahead across the fields and a drive, passing **Duddle Farm** on the left. Cross a bridge and stile down into a field. Go straight on and bear left, following the track round the hill. Cross a stile by a converted barn and walk up the drive. At the fingerpost keep straight on through a gate, signed 'Lower Bockhampton'. Bear left through another gate then walk down the field to a gate at the far corner. Go through and straight on, with the river on your left. Go through the farmyard to the road.

④ Turn left by **Bridge Cottage**. Cross the stream and immediately turn right, on to a causeway. After ½ mile (800m) turn right, signed 'Stinsford'. Walk up and turn left into the churchyard, just below the church. Pass the **church** to your left, and the Hardy graves to your right. Leave by the top gate and walk up the road. Pass a piggery and turn right along the road. Turn left at the end to the main road by a house.

⑤ Turn right, up the road. After the entrance to **Birkin House**, bear left through a gate and immediately turn right on to a path through woodland, parallel with the road. Descend, cross a stile and bear left to a fingerpost. Next, go through the gate and bear diagonally right up the field, signposted 'Higher Bockhampton'. At the top corner keep straight on through a gate and turn right towards a barn. Pass this and bear right on a track to the road. Turn left, then right by the post box, and right again to return to the car park.

WHAT TO LOOK FOR i

As you turn up from the watercourse towards Stinsford church, look left for the unusual sight of **pictorial thatch**. What looks like a bear and other animals have been carved into the newly thatched roofs of a cottage and its garage. In the churchyard look out for the big slate tombstone of Poet Laureate Cecil Day-Lewis (1904–72), who also wrote popular detective novels under the pseudonym Nicholas Blake.

WHERE TO EAT AND DRINK i

The **Greenwood** tea rooms and restaurant occupy a beautifully restored, thatched barn, right beside the car park. The restaurant is part of Greenwood Grange Farm self-catering complex, converted from barns built by Hardy's father. Benches and tables outside overlook a landscaped garden and pond. Inside it's light and airy, with a central fire in winter. The food is freshly cooked and there are delicious chocolate cakes and pastries to have with your tea. Children are very welcome, but dogs must stay outside.

The White Horse at Osmington

Where the world saw a sane King George III take a well-earned break.

•DISTANCE•	4 miles (6.4km)
•MINIMUM TIME•	2hrs
•ASCENT / GRADIENT•	568ft (173m) ▲▲▲
•LEVEL OF DIFFICULTY•	林林 林
•PATHS•	Farm and village lanes, woodland paths, field paths, 9 stiles
•LANDSCAPE•	Sheltered green valley behind coastline and chalky ridge of White Horse Hill
•SUGGESTED MAP•	aqua3 OS Explorer OL 15 Purbeck & South Dorset
•START / FINISH•	Grid reference: SY 724829
•DOG FRIENDLINESS•	No problems
•PARKING•	Church Lane in Osmington, just off A353
•PUBLIC TOILETS•	None on route

BACKGROUND TO THE WALK

The 1994 film *The Madness of King George* did much to remind the world of a monarch whose identity had been obscured by time. In the Dorset town of Weymouth, however, he has never been forgotten.

Weymouth is a trading port with a patchy history, including the first outbreak on English shores of the Black Death (► Walk 32), and a proximity to France that had left it vulnerable to raids. The town found new life in the 18th century as a base for trade with the Americas and the shipping of convicts to Australia. The 1780s saw the emergence of the popular cult of sea bathing (and even seawater drinking) – Weymouth joined in. A royal visit in 1789, however, was to rocket the little town into the top rank of seaside resorts.

Holiday Spin

Rumours of George III's mental instability were threatening to destabilise the country. Accordingly, it decided that the King should go on a short and highly visible tour, to enable his subjects to see how much better he was. Weymouth was picked, and a six day journey commenced for the royal party, which consisted of the King, the Queen and the three princesses. It was a great build-up and, by the time they reached Weymouth, the crowds were ecstatic, with bunting, mayoral receptions and gunships firing salutes in the bay. The King responded to their warmth with a short walk-about on his very first evening and the declaration that he 'never saw a sight so pleasing'.

Patriotic Band

Any hopes that the King might have had of a quiet dip in the sea, however, were dashed a week later by the strength and volume of local enthusiasm for their royal visitor. Even as his royal-crested bathing hut was being wheeled into the sea, a band hidden in a nearby bathing machine were waiting to burst into a loyal song as soon as the regal body hit the water. George III spent ten weeks here on his first visit, enjoying day trips to Lulworth, Milton

Abbey and St Adhelm's Head, and sailing off Portland. The royal family returned two years later for a holiday and then returned every year until 1805.

In 1808 John Rainier (brother of the heroic Rear Admiral Peter Rainier, whose name was given to Mount Rainier near Seattle), arranged for a symbol of the town's undying loyalty and gratitude for the royal attention bestowed upon them, to be carved into the chalk downs above Osmington. And so an elegant silhouette of the King on horseback was created, around 324ft (99m) high, riding away from the town – presumably in a much healthier condition after his vacation. Once clearly visible from Weymouth, Portland and ships out at sea, today the chalk figure is weathered and grey, but you can still pick out the graceful lines of the horse's legs and tail, and the King's distinctive cocked hat.

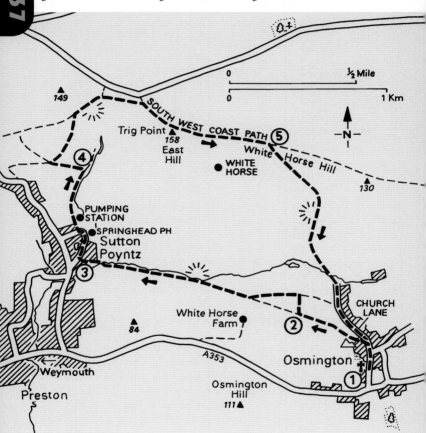

Walk 37 Directions

① From **Osmington church** walk down the village street of pretty thatched cottages. At the junction keep on down **Church Lane**. Opposite **Forge Barn**, at the end of

a wall, turn left up a long, steep flight of steps, signed 'Sutton Poyntz'. The path rises through woodland. After a second set of steps bear right on the path which undulates through the trees. Cross a stile and continue straight on to the end of a field.

Walk 37

② Cross a stile and turn immediately right to cross a second stile and walk down the field. Turn left through a gate and head straight across the field. Cross a farm track and bear ahead and right. Cross a pair of stiles and continue along the bottom of the field, looking to your right to see the **White Horse**. Continue though a gap. At the end of the next field bear left, through a gateway, then go straight on (yellow marker), towards **Sutton Poyntz**. Soon veer right, cross a stream and bear left through a gate. Follow the path to a stile and continue to the road.

③ Turn right, pass the **Mill House** and the tall, red brick mill on the left. Pass the village pond and the **Springhead** pub on the right. Bear left and right up a lane by **Springfield Cottage**. Go through a gate and follow the track straight

ahead. Go through another gate, with a pumping station on the right, below the bottom of the steep combe where the spring emerges.

④ Cross a stile by a gate and turn left up the grassy lane. About half-way up the hill turn right, up a track (the upper of two) that leads to the top above the combe, with great views along the valley and down to **Weymouth Bay** and **Portland**. Keep right on the green track, go through a gate and keep left along the field edge. Follow the path round to the right and walk up the field (a lane soon joins from the left). Stay on this track past the trig point. Go through a gate and keep straight on, with a good view to strip lynchets on the hillside ahead.

⑤ Go through a gate and bear down to the right, signed 'Osmington'. The track leads down the hill, through a gate – look back to see the White Horse again. Follow the lane back up through the village to your car.

Dorset's Other Hardy

A long walk over rolling farmland from a high vantage point above Abbotsbury, where Nelson's fighting companion is remembered.

•DISTANCE•	7 miles (11.3km)
•MINIMUM TIME•	3hrs 30min
•ASCENT / GRADIENT•	784ft (228m) ▲▲▲
•LEVEL OF DIFFICULTY•	👫 👫 👫
•PATHS•	Field tracks, quiet roads, woodland tracks, 10 stiles
•LANDSCAPE•	Rolling hills and escarpments above Abbotsbury
•SUGGESTED MAP•	aqua3 OS Explorer OL15 Purbeck & South Dorset
•START / FINISH•	Grid reference: SY 312876
•DOG FRIENDLINESS•	Some unfriendly stiles, some road walking
•PARKING•	By Hardy Monument, signed off road between Portesham and Winterbourne Abbas
•PUBLIC TOILETS•	None on route; nearest in Back Street, Abbotsbury

BACKGROUND TO THE WALK

Admiral Hardy is best remembered today as the close friend of Admiral Lord Horatio Nelson, who attended the great naval hero in the hour of his death after the Battle of Trafalgar. He was a hero in his own right, his features decorating jugs and tankards of the time. Compared to his literary namesake, you'll find few signboards and memorials to this Hardy in his home county, but there is one monument – and it's a big one.

The Sea in his Veins

Thomas Masterman Hardy was born in 1769 at Kingston Russell, near Long Bredy, and from the age of nine raised at Portesham House in Portesham, a practical sort of village tucked well back under the hill of Black Down. At 12 he got his first taste of life at sea, but was sent home for further schooling. After three more years on land he escaped to sea again, this time slipping secretly aboard a merchantman, where he served before the mast and in the galley before enlisting. His naval career was to be illustrious.

In 1796 he had been put in charge of a captured foreign vessel when he witnessed two frigates under the command of Nelson in severe and imminent danger from a Spanish squadron. In a courageous and selfless act, Hardy hoisted the British flag, drawing the Spanish fire to his own vessel. He was captured in the ensuing fracas, but was later returned to the Royal Navy in an exchange of prisoners. Some months later he and Nelson were involved in another near-death adventure, when Nelson stopped the flight of his ship to wait for Hardy, who had gone to the rescue of a drowning seaman. His bold action so surprised his Spanish pursuers that they stopped in their tracks.

Brothers in Arms

The friendship of the two men was to be deep and lasting. Hardy became the captain of Nelson's flagships and served with him at many of his most famous battles, including the Nile in 1798. In 1805, as captain of HMS *Victory*, he was at Nelson's side in that man's greatest hour and, when Nelson was mortally wounded, Hardy took command of the fleet.

Nelson's last words were a blessing addressed to his great friend. Hardy continued in his career and stayed in the navy for another 30 years. His final service was as Governor of Greenwich Hospital, where he died and was buried in 1839.

Solid and Reliable

Set high on Black Down hill, the Hardy Monument, solid and reliable as Hardy himself, looks like a Victorian chimney. You can climb up inside on summer weekends, but even if it is closed, the views from here over a sea of green fields and on down to Portland are superb.

Walk 38 Directions

① Turn left down a path by the entrance, signposted 'Inland Route'. Follow the broad track down through the woods. At the bottom turn right and bear left, before a gate, over a stile. Walk up the edge of two fields. At the corner go over

a stone stile and immediately cross another. Walk alongside the fence to the hedge.

② Turn left on to the road and right towards a farm. After passing the farm bear left through a gate and go up a track, then through another gate and bear right. Pass **Hampton Stone Circle** and keep

Walk 38

straight on. Cross a stile and bear along the fence and down some steps, signposted 'West Bexington'. Follow the path along the hillside and up through a gate to a road.

③ Turn right and take the first road left. (Turn left here for Walk 39.) Soon bear right along a track. Go through a gate (blue marker) and walk ahead down the hedge (aircraft fly very low here, so beware). Keep straight on through three fields.

④ Go through a gate to a junction of tracks (Walk 39 rejoins from the left). Bear right across the field, passing **Kingston Russell Stone Circle**. Go through a gate and bear slightly left over the hill, passing earthworks on the left. At the bottom go straight on down to a gate. Go through and bear left, then go through a gate to your right and down the hill.

WHAT TO LOOK FOR ℹ
There are two **stone circles** on this route, their purpose and origin obscure. The first is Hampton Stone Circle, where the nine flinty stone lumps (they look like concrete aggregate) are well used by cattle as scratching posts. The stone is a natural phenomenon, with flint gravel cemented by silica, laid down over 40 million years ago. The more numerous lumps of the Kingston Russell Stone Circle are mottled with lichen.

⑤ In the middle of the field turn right. Cross a footbridge to go through a gate. Cross a stream and walk straight ahead up the field. Bear left along the hedge. Cross a double stile and head diagonally left. Cross another footbridge over a stream. Turn right, bear left up through some trees, then go up to the right, to a stile. Cross and go

WHERE TO EAT AND DRINK ℹ
Abbotsbury is well supplied with tea rooms, some of which are passed on Walk 39. On Market Street the **Bakehouse Tearoom** (also an antique and collectables shop) offers home-made cakes including great wedges of Dorset apple cake. The **Wheelwrights Tearoom**, also on the route, offers tasty light lunches (and has an art gallery too). If you want something stronger, the **Ilchester Arms Hotel** has an extensive beer garden.

over the hill towards **Littlebredy**. Cross a stile by a fingerpost and go straight on. Pass the church, go left through a gate and turn right on to the road. Bear right at the junction, passing **Bridehead** house. Continue past **Littlebredy Farm** and up a long hill. At the junction turn right.

⑥ Soon bear left on a bridleway to follow the track beside some woods. Cross the road and go straight ahead. Descend through the woods and, where the track divides, turn up to the right. After ½ mile (800m), before the road, turn right and right again on to a footpath. Cross a bridge and follow the woodland path up to the left. Stay on this to reach the road opposite the **Hardy Monument**.

WHILE YOU'RE THERE ℹ
Abbotsbury Swannery is a unique sanctuary. Mute swans have lived on the Fleet for 600 years, since they were introduced as a food source for the abbey, and their nest site is now protected. Come in April to see them nesting and from mid-May to see cygnets. In the huge tithe barn near by **Smuggling Adventure** offers fun for the under 11s, with a themed play area and a farm where children can cuddle rabbits and pet pigs, drive a toy tractor and go for pony rides.

Abbotsbury Loop

Extend Walk 38 to visit an attractive village of golden stone.
See map and information panel for Walk 38

•DISTANCE•	9 miles (14.5km)
•MINIMUM TIME•	5hrs
•ASCENT / GRADIENT•	1,388ft (423m) ▲▲▲
•LEVEL OF DIFFICULTY•	🚶🚶 🚶🚶 🚶🚶

Walk 39 Directions (Walk 38 option)

At Point ③ on Walk 38 turn left and soon bear right through a gate on to a bridleway, signed 'West Bexington and Abbotsbury'. Keep straight ahead along the line of the fence. At the brow of the hill go through the gate and continue downhill, following a track in the grass. Go through a gate and carry on down. Below lies **Abbotsbury**, a lovely village of golden stone, sheltered from the sea by the Fleet and dominated in the landscape by the solitary **St Catherine's Chapel**, alone on its hill. An abbey was founded here in the time of King Cnut. Dissolution in the 16th century left it with a cathedral, one of the biggest tithe barns in England, and a unique swannery.

At a crossroads of tracks keep straight on, signed 'Abbotsbury'. Go through a gate on to the road and turn right, down into the village, Point Ⓐ. Take the first lane left and turn right at the bottom along the high street. Turn right up **Market Street** (a left turn here leads to the **Swannery**), passing the **Ilchester Arms Hotel** on the left and various small galleries. Bear right opposite,

along **Back Street**. Turn left up **Blind Lane**, just before **Spring Cottage**, and follow the track as it hooks back above the village then turns sharply uphill on a path that is the same orange colour as the houses. Go through a gate, then continue up the track. At the signpost keep straight on. Go through a gate and continue straight up. Just before the limestone crest go through another gate and bear right, signed 'Hardy Monument'. Walk diagonally up the hill through hummocks, Point Ⓑ.

At the top, by a fingerpost, cross a stile and bear left up the edge of the field, signed 'Macmillan Way'. Go through a gate in the top corner, on through another gate, and down a farm track. Meet a road at the bottom and turn left. Follow this along the peaceful wooded valley, descending to **Gorwell Farm**. Pass the farm on your left and keep straight on. Next, pass **Sundial Cottage** on the right and bear left through a gate, again signed 'Macmillan Way'. Turn sharp right, uphill. Go through the gate on your left and walk alongside the hedge line, through a second gate and then ahead. Go through another gate and reach a junction of tracks. This is Point ④ on Walk 38. Bear left across the field.

Walk 40

Mysterious Moonfleet

Exploring the strange panorama of land and water behind Chesil Beach.

•DISTANCE•	6 miles (9.7km)
•MINIMUM TIME•	2hrs 30min
•ASCENT / GRADIENT•	430ft (131m)
•LEVEL OF DIFFICULTY•	
•PATHS•	Coastal path (slippery after rain), country lanes, 11 stiles
•LANDSCAPE•	Low hills and secretive villages inland from Chesil Beach
•SUGGESTED MAP•	aqua3 OS Explorer OL 15 Purbeck & South Dorset
•START / FINISH•	Grid reference: SY 619807
•DOG FRIENDLINESS•	Keep under close control around wildlife
•PARKING•	Lay-by, near gateway by Moonfleet Manor Hotel
•PUBLIC TOILETS•	None on route

Walk 40 Directions

Cross the stile at the lay-by to walk down the field towards the Fleet, signed 'Coastal Path'. Pass the **Moonfleet Manor Hotel** on your right, cross a stile and continue down. Turn right through a gate. Descend steps into some trees to cross a bridge and stile. Continue past the hotel, with the shell of a boathouse on the left.

There's something eerie about the Fleet lagoon, trapped by a high bank of sighing golden shingle. John Meade Falkner captured the mysterious atmosphere in his popular 1898 adventure novel about

---

WHERE TO EAT AND DRINK ⓘ
Moonfleet Manor Hotel, a haven of understated, old world charm and polished parquet floors, extends a gracious welcome to families (and dogs). Take lunch or afternoon tea in the Verandah Restaurant, overlooking the Fleet. At Langton Herring the **Elm Tree Inn** welcomes walkers, and has a sunny beer garden (no dogs allowed inside).

---

smugglers and kidnapping, *Moonfleet*. Moonfleet is a corruption of Mohun (► Walk 26), and gives its name to a handsome but isolated Georgian hotel on the inland shore. One of its nicknames is Dead Man's Bay, a grim reflection of the many lives that have been lost in shipwrecks here, for on the seaward side of the bank the water is deep and treacherous. Wrecks include the *Hope* of Amsterdam, which caused mayhem in 1748 when it sank, because gold and silver were washed ashore.

Cross a bridge and stile in the wall and pass **Gore Cove** on the left. Cross a stile to the right and walk inland along the wall. Bear right through a gate on to a lane. Follow this up the hill to **Langton Herring**, walking on pink granite chippings. Go through a gate and down to **Fleet Way Cottage**. Turn right, down the lane, and continue straight ahead, with the **Elm Tree** pub on the left. Retrace your route, passing the hotel again. At the gate turn right along the fence, with the wedge of **Portland** ahead. Go

Walk 40

through a gate and continue along the field edge. Beware of passing racehorses from **Sea Barn Farm**, up the hill on the left, which train on the gallop beside you. Pass some old pill-boxes.

Chesil Bank is a storm beach, stretching 17 miles (27km) from Bridport's West Bay down to the cliffs at Portland. The stones that form it were deposited into the Channel by meltwater after the last Ice Age and washed back towards the land by the relentless motion of the waves. The stones are graded in size, from pea-sized gravel at the western end to hefty cobbles at Portland. It is said that local sailors washed ashore or smugglers landing their booty in the dark could tell their exact whereabouts by the size of the pebbles beneath their feet.

The path curves in round **Butterstreet Cove**. Turn right, down some steps that run through wind-blown hawthorn. Cross a footbridge and stile. Continue to cross a stile by a gate and bear round to the left, towards the tiny hamlet of **East Fleet**.

This was the scene in 1824 of dreadful destruction, when Chesil Bank was breached. In a violent storm the sea swept over the top.

The village was washed away, leaving nothing but the chancel of the church. That still exists, containing memorials to the Mohun family, and a few houses that were rebuilt around it. The Fleet itself is some 8 miles (13km) long. The muddy shallows benefit from vast underwater pastures of long, wavy eelgrass – great food for birds and habitat for a variety of other marine life, including pipe fish and sticklebacks. Even in winter, when it dies back and is washed up along the water line like scrambled cassette tape, it's a refuge for little green shore crabs.

Bear right over a footbridge, passing what's left of the church on the left. Cross a stile by a gate and go straight ahead, past a row of cottages, to the road. Turn left and follow this uphill into the village of **Fleet Common**. Pass the newer church of pinkish stone and stay on this road for another ½ mile (800m) to a junction. Go straight ahead, passing a Victorian post box on your left, then go through the manorial gateway with its stone lions. The sea now comes back into view. Follow the road down through woods and past several houses, to return to your car. The road continues, curving left, to end at the **Moonfleet Manor Hotel**.

In the Doghouse at Purse Caundle

Over hill and valley from a village dominated by a fine manor house.

•DISTANCE•	5 miles (8km)
•MINIMUM TIME•	2hrs
•ASCENT / GRADIENT•	427ft (130m) ▲▲▲
•LEVEL OF DIFFICULTY•	🚶 🚶 🚶
•PATHS•	Muddy field paths, farm tracks, country roads, wet bridleway (wellies recommended), 13 stiles
•LANDSCAPE•	Little green hills and valleys with scattered settlements
•SUGGESTED MAP•	aqua3 OS Explorer 129 Yeovil & Sherborne
•START / FINISH•	Grid reference: ST 695175
•DOG FRIENDLINESS•	Some road walking
•PARKING•	Limited space by war memorial, Purse Caundle
•PUBLIC TOILETS•	None on route

BACKGROUND TO THE WALK

On the north Dorset border, Purse Caundle is reached via a narrow road from the busy A30, and too easily bypassed by folk in a hurry to reach Sherborne. It is an ordinary little village with an extraordinarily fine manor house. On the village lane you are almost too close to admire it properly – you get a better overall view of its extent from the hillside opposite, towards the end of this walk.

Ghostly Hounds

The present manor dates from the early 15th century. It is said to be haunted by various spirits of its rich past. For example, if you're passing this way on Midsummer Eve, you may hear the ghostly howling of a pack of hounds. They are giving tongue on the scent, no doubt, of a ghostly stag. The explanation is simple enough. In the 13th century the lodge house here was a dogs' home. More accurately, it was a haven where royal hunting dogs, wounded in the chase in the deer forests of Blackmoor, could be brought for rest and recovery under the personal care of the steward, John Godwyne.

Royal Whims

For this important service Godwyne was granted the manor of Purse Caundle. Such whimsical royal patronage was not untypical in Dorset. On a similar basis, the manor of Winfrith was granted to the man who held the King's washbasin on His Royal Highness's birthday, and that of Kingston Russell to a widow who was responsible for putting the King's chess pieces back in the box when His Majesty had finished playing. The manor, presumably minus the dogs, was eventually sold on for the handsome price of 100 silver marks to a Richard Long, who started building the present structure around 1429.

Another ghost apparently lived in an old well and made his presence known by chasing ladies upstairs. When that all got too much, the well was filled in and the staircase dismantled. Robbed of his fun, the ghost was seen no more.

Walk 41

Great Chamber

From the outside, in daylight, the manor house looks mellow enough today, guarded by a big stone boar on the driveway. The slim oriel window overlooking the road conceals the Great Chamber and there's a splendid beamed roof in the Great Hall. It has changed hands many times through the centuries, most notably during the Civil War, when William Hanham, whose carved initials proclaim him responsible for much of the later building of the house, unfortunately picked the losing side and lost everything to the Commonwealth. The manor is still privately owned, but is occasionally opened to the public – see it if you can.

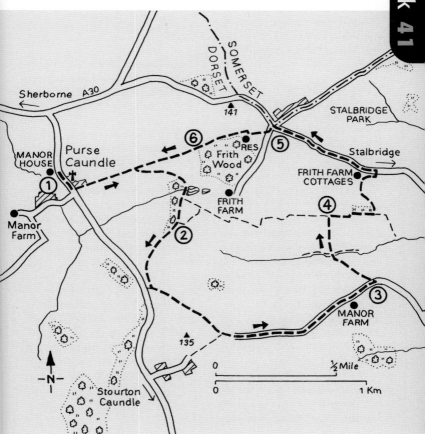

Walk 41 Directions

① Park by the church where there is a **memorial bench** in honour of four local men who were killed in the First World War. Walk up the village street to admire the manor house. Return, pass the phone box and turn left through a gate. Go straight up the edge of the field, cross a stile and turn right to continue on this line, up through a gateway and across another field. After a second gateway bear right up the field. Cross a stile in the corner and turn right. Soon cross a stile and pass a lake to your left. Cross the stile at the far side and bear right along the field edge.

Walk 41

② Cross a stile at the corner and go on down the edge of the field. The path curves down and up to a gate. Go through this gate and swing left, up a bridleway. This narrows and is shared with a stream. Go through a gate and keep straight on up the hill. Go through a gate in the top corner and follow the muddy track. This becomes a hedged lane, which you follow for ½ mile (800m) to pass **Manor Farm**. Continue through a gate.

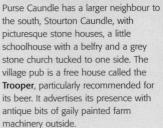

> **WHERE TO EAT AND DRINK** ⓘ
> Purse Caundle has a larger neighbour to the south, Stourton Caundle, with picturesque stone houses, a little schoolhouse with a belfry and a grey stone church tucked to one side. The village pub is a free house called the **Trooper**, particularly recommended for its beer. It advertises its presence with antique bits of gaily painted farm machinery outside.

> **WHAT TO LOOK FOR** ⓘ
> The massive encircling wall of **Stalbridge Park**, silvered with lichen, creates an eager expectation of a glimpse of a great house. It's an anticipation fed by the massive gateway beside the road to the north of Stalbridge. You'll peer in vain, however, for the mansion was demolished in 1822 and never replaced.

③ Turn left at the fingerpost over a stile. Bear left down the field to cross three stiles and a footbridge in the middle of the hedge. Head diagonally left down the next field. Cross a pair of stiles and a footbridge in the corner and immediately turn right over a stile and a footbridge. Walk straight ahead up the field edge.

④ At the top turn right, then bear right along the bottom of a young plantation. Go through a gateway and turn left up the edge of a field. Follow the path round behind **Frith**

> **WHILE YOU'RE THERE** ⓘ
> Drop into **Stalbridge** for a selection of pleasant-looking pubs and to admire the 15th-century village cross, which holds up the traffic on the long, narrow high street. Tall and slim and golden, its features are well worn by time. The cross head is a modern replica – the original fell off in 1950.

Farm Cottages, down to a gate. Turn left on the road and walk up it for ½ mile (800m), beside the stone wall of **Stalbridge Park**.

⑤ At a crossroads turn left, towards **Frith Farm**. Soon bear right, following markers. The path then bends left, through a gate to a covered reservoir. Pass this and turn right, through a gate. Descend some steps and bear left down the edge of the field, with views to the manor. Continue straight on through a gap.

⑥ At the bottom bear left into woodland (but not through the gate). Walk down this ridge, then cross the ditch on the left and continue down the edge of the field. Go through a gateway and retrace your route to the **church**.

Raleigh's Country Retreat at Sherborne

A gentle circuit around Sherborne, the sometime home of a cut-and-thrust regal pirate, politician and poet who courted danger.

•DISTANCE•	6½ miles (10.4km)
•MINIMUM TIME•	3hrs
•ASCENT / GRADIENT•	443ft (135m) ▲ ▲ ▲
•LEVEL OF DIFFICULTY•	🚶 🚶 🚶
•PATHS•	Country lanes, green lane, field paths, estate tracks, 9 stiles
•LANDSCAPE•	Gentle hills and dairy villages south of Sherborne, open parkland, woodland
•SUGGESTED MAP•	aqua3 OS Explorer 129 Yeovil & Sherborne
•START / FINISH•	Grid reference: ST 670157
•DOG FRIENDLINESS•	Some road walking
•PARKING•	On road by church, Haydon village, 2 miles (3.2km) south east of Sherborne
•PUBLIC TOILETS•	None on route

BACKGROUND TO THE WALK

Sir Walter Raleigh was an adventurer-cum-pirate, navigator, courtier and poet. His lasting legacies to modern daily life are the, nowadays humble, staples of tobacco and potatoes. A Devon man, born in 1552, he came to the attention of Queen Elizabeth I. Consequently he sailed off to the Americas to claim new lands for her and to plunder Spanish treasure ships along the way. By the time he returned, in 1587, his light at court was being outshone by the youthful 2nd Earl of Essex.

Courting Danger

Raleigh, now around 40, fell madly in love with the much younger Elizabeth Throckmorton, the Queen's maid of honour. She became pregnant and they married in secret. When the Queen found out, she was furious and imprisoned them both in the Tower of London briefly, before banishing them from her sight.

Raleigh had earlier acquired the Norman castle at Sherborne, formerly owned by the Bishop of Salisbury. He moved there with Elizabeth and their child but the old castle proved inadequate. In 1594 he built a new, fashionably square house with corner towers on the opposite river bank. He constructed water gardens and a bowling green, planted exotic trees brought back from his travels and entertained London friends. It is said he loved Sherborne 'above all his possessions, of all places on earth'.

But he went to sea again, this time to explore the coast of Trinidad and the Orinoco, joining in the sack of Cadiz in 1596. His role as Governor of Jersey in North America took him away from home again in 1600. In 1603, perceived as a threat to the new monarch after the death of Elizabeth, Raleigh was sentenced to death. This was commuted to life imprisonment and, after 13 years in the Tower (which he spent writing poetry and compiling a history of the world), he was released to return to the Orinoco in search of gold, now accompanied by his son, Wat. Despite explicit instructions from James I not to attack the Spanish (except in self-defence), some men under Raleigh's command near the Orinoco River did just that. Furthermore, his son was killed in the skirmish. On his return, Raleigh had to carry the can – the 1603 treason charge was revived.

On 19 October 1618 Sir Walter Raleigh ate a hearty breakfast and took tobacco. Cavalier and poetic to the last, he refused a blindfold and asked to see the executioner's axe, saying, 'This is a sharp Medicine, but it is a Physician for all Diseases'. His body was buried in nearby St Margaret's, Westminster. As was then the custom, his wife was given his embalmed head, a worthy 'conversation piece'. Thereafter it was, apparently, her constant companion. The head was finally buried next to the rest of him. Since Sir Walter's time Sherborne Castle has been enlarged and modified, partly by the Digby family. Today it is a charming mansion in a spectacular lakeside setting, ringed by woods and open parkland.

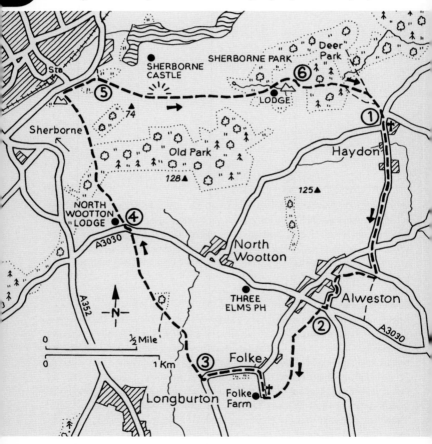

Walk 42 **Directions**

① With the **church** on your left, walk down the road and out of Haydon. At the junction continue

ahead, signposted 'Bishop's Caundle'. At the minor junction cross the stile, straight ahead. Turn right, up the field edge, towards **Alweston**. Cross a stile and bear diagonally left over the field. Cross a stile in the corner, go down a path and keep straight on down the road, which curves round to meet the **A3030**.

WHILE YOU'RE THERE ⓘ

Sherborne itself is dominated by the huge square tower of the **Abbey Church**, on Half Moon Street. Admire its saw-tooth Norman entrance and outstanding fan-vaulted roof. Exploring the streets on foot you'll find a buttermarket, old yarn mills and a jumble of low houses and little golden terraces, all on a tiny scale. Look out for the lovely Georgian square of Newland Gardens.

---

② Turn right, then soon turn left over a stile in the hedge. Go straight over the field to a gap. Bear diagonally right over the next field. About half-way along the far side go through the hedge via a stile at a corner (yellow marker). Continue straight ahead along the hedge, crossing several stiles and footbridges. Continue along the wall towards **Folke church**. Cross two stiles, go through a gate and turn right up the lane into the village, passing the church entrance and a raised pavement on the right. Keep left at the junction, then follow the lane as it bends round to the left.

③ Follow the road as it bends sharply left, then turn right up the signed bridleway. Follow this for a mile (1.6km), gently ascending. It becomes broader and muddier, reaching the main road via a gate.

④ Turn left then right through the gate directly beside the lodge, up a lane. Continue straight on down through some woods, with the park wall to your right. Where the drive sweeps right by a cottage, keep straight on, up a track, passing

sports fields on the left. Go through two gates, cross a road and go through another gate by a lodge on to a tarmac track. Follow this down a steep gorge to meet the main road. Take the path immediately right, through a gate, and walk up the hill above the **castle gateway**.

⑤ Pass through a gate into **Sherborne Park**. Follow the grassy track straight ahead, downhill. Go through a kissing gate and straight ahead on an estate track, with superb views of the castle. Go up the track to a thatched lodge. Here go through the wooden gate and up the hill.

WHAT TO LOOK FOR ⓘ

The battlemented **Church of St Lawrence** at Folke dates from 1628. If it is locked, walk round and peer through the windows for sight of the massive, carved, Jacobean chancel screen.

---

⑥ At the top keep right, through another gate into the woods. Follow the track round. Keep straight on to a tarmac path and pass a huge barn on the left. Follow the track right, and go straight on at the junction. Descend to a **lodge**. Now go through the gate and straight on to return to your car.

WHERE TO EAT AND DRINK ⓘ

The **Three Elms** pub at North Wootton offers an extensive menu of freshly prepared food and five real ales on tap at a time. The landlord collects models of classic cars – and his display cases line the walls. Try home-made faggots with mashed potato and mushy peas, a burger topped with Dorset Blue Vinney cheese or the wide selection of sandwich fillings. Dogs, children and walkers all receive a friendly welcome, but leave your muddy boots by the door.

Giant Steps to Cerne Abbas

A valley walk from Minterne Magna to see a famous chalk hill carving.

•**DISTANCE**•	5½ miles (8.8km)
•**MINIMUM TIME**•	2hrs 30min
•**ASCENT / GRADIENT**•	591ft (180m) ▲▲▲
•**LEVEL OF DIFFICULTY**•	👥 👥 👥
•**PATHS**•	Country paths and tracks, minor road, main road, 2 stiles
•**LANDSCAPE**•	Head of Cerne Valley, scattered with old settlements
•**SUGGESTED MAP**•	aqua3 OS Explorer 117 Cerne Abbas & Bere Regis
•**START / FINISH**•	Grid reference: ST 659043
•**DOG FRIENDLINESS**•	Lead essential on main road stretches
•**PARKING**•	Car park (free) opposite church in Minterne Magna
•**PUBLIC TOILETS**•	Cerne Abbas

BACKGROUND TO THE WALK

The chalk outline of the Cerne Abbas Giant is so familiar that the reality, seen from the hillside opposite rather than above from the air, is a surprise. His proportions change at this shallower angle, and this of course is how he was designed to be seen – all 180ft (55m) of him. Quite when he was made, and by whom, is part of his mystery.

Was he drawn up there by the Romans, a portrait of the demi-god Hercules? Could he be part of a cunning neolithic plan to frighten away potential enemies from a settlement on the hilltop? On the other hand he might be of Celtic origin, for the giant has been linked to a pan handle discovered 12 miles (19km) away on Hod Hill. Made of bronze, it depicts a naked man clutching a club in one hand and a limp hare in the other. The man has wings and is surrounded by other symbols which identify him as Nodens, a Celtic god of healing and fertility. His features and the angle of his legs suggest close resemblance to the Giant, and place him in the 1st century AD. Whatever the truth of it, the Giant has been seen as a symbol of fertility for many centuries. It used to be seen as the acceptable thing for childless women to spend a night of hope on his crotch. The fencing now around the Giant is to prevent him from being eroded away.

St Augustine visited Cerne and preached to the locals on the spot now marked by St Augustine's Well. A verse on the wall there records how he offered two shepherds the choice of something to drink, beer or water. When they primly asked for water, the saint rewarded them with a brewery. An abbey was founded here in AD 987. Its most famous inhabitant, Aelfric, produced a number of schoolbooks in Anglo-Saxon. A Latin primer, in which pupils adopt the characters of working people, such as a shoemaker and a fowler, and describe their lives to their teacher, is a fascinating record of daily life. The abbey was dissolved in 1539, along with Dorset's other monastic houses, but an imposing gatehouse with overhanging oriel window and carved lions remains, along with other venerable buildings, including an ancient hospital, set around a flowered courtyard.

The village of Cerne Abbas is a lovely mixture of old houses, some half-timbered, some stone, with flint, thatch and brick in evidence. The Red Lion Hotel claims to be one of 13 original public houses and if that seems excessive in a place this size, it should be explained that Cerne was once a major staging post on the coaching routes.

Walk 43

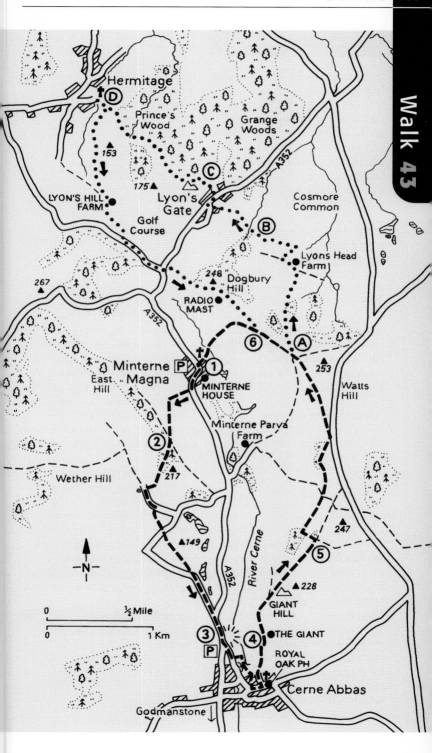

Walk 43

Walk 43 Directions

① Turn right and walk up the road through the village. Where it curls left, turn right through a gate on to a bridleway and go straight ahead up the hill. At the top go through a gate and bear left. Follow the blue marker diagonally up to the right. Go through a gate, walk on past some trees, then bend up, round a field towards the tree line.

② Go through the gap and take the track down diagonally left through the woods. At the bottom turn left along the road. After a bend take the footpath right, across the field. After a line of trees veer left, towards a white gate. Cross a road, pass to the right of a gate, and continue straight on down the field. Pass another white gate then continue ahead on the road. At the end bear right on to the **A352**.

> ### WHAT TO LOOK FOR
> Hidden from the main road behind high stone walls, **Minterne House** is a large, yellow, Victorian pile, built by the Digby family. It is not open to the public, but its magnificent gardens are. Paths weave through a famous collection of rhododendrons and magnolias.

③ Soon cross to the car park for the best view of the Giant. Take the road down to the village and turn left, signposted 'Pottery'. Turn right by the stream, signposted 'Village Centre'. Continue over a slab bridge and pass an old mill. Bear left, to the high street. Turn left, and left again in front of the **Royal Oak**, to the church. Walk up the **Old Pitch Market** to the **Abbey**. Turn right into the churchyard and bear left. Go through a gate, signposted 'Giant's Hill', and bear left.

④ Cross a stile, then turn right up some steps. Now follow the path to the left, round the contour of the hill, below a fence. As the path divides, keep right, up the hill, towards the top. Bear left along the ridge, cross a stile by a fingerpost and head diagonally right, towards a barn.

> ### WHERE TO EAT AND DRINK
> The **Royal Oak** in Cerne Abbas is an old free house where you can get steak and fresh salads, Portland crab sandwiches and Dorset apple cake. The **Singing Kettle Tearoom** has a garden at the back and doubles as a gift shop.

⑤ At the barn turn left and go down through a gate. Soon turn right and follow the bridleway along the hillside, with views to Minterne Parva. Keep straight ahead at a junction of tracks, then dip down through a gateway above some woods. Keep straight on to go through a gate near the road. Turn left along the grassy track. At a gateway turn left on to a gravel lane (soon turn right for Walk 44).

⑥ Directly above **Minterne House** (Walk 44 rejoins here), turn left through a small gate and bear left. Go through a gate and turn left, downhill. Continue down through several gates and keep right at the fingerpost down a broad track. Cross the stream, then walk up past the church to return to the car park.

> ### WHILE YOU'RE THERE
> Explore nearby **Godmanstone**, where the Smiths Arms claims to be the smallest pub in England. It is said that Charles II was passing one day and stopped at the forge to ask for a drink. Informed by the blacksmith that he could not oblige as he had no licence, the King promptly granted him one.

Hermitage Treasures

A hilly loop to a church that provided wartime refuge for art treasures.
See map and information panel for Walk 43

•DISTANCE•	11¼ miles (18.1km)
•MINIMUM TIME•	5hrs 30min
•ASCENT / GRADIENT•	1,264ft (385m) ▲▲▲
•LEVEL OF DIFFICULTY•	🚶🚶 🚶🚶 🚶🚶

Walk 44 Directions (Walk 43 option)

From the gravel lane turn right through a gate, Point Ⓐ, and bear diagonally left down a field. Join a farm track and continue downhill. At a junction by a house turn left, signed 'Bridgeway'. Descend to cross a stream, go up some steps and cross a stile. Bear straight over the field to a gate. Walk up the broad track between fences. Now zig-zag down to the gate at the bottom right-hand corner, then go back up, diagonally left. Go through a gap and bear right over the brow of the hill. Go through a gate, Point Ⓑ.

Cross a footbridge and bear ahead and right, towards a scrapyard. Go through a gate at the top right-hand corner. Head down the field, but soon bear left through a gap and then diagonally down to the far corner, below some stables. Go through a pair of gates and follow the track to the road, in **Lyon's Gate**. Keep right, on to the **A352**. Soon cross and turn left up a bridleway into some woods.

Look for a lake on the right, then take the path on the left between trees (Point Ⓒ). Go through a gate,

turn right and follow the zig-zag track uphill, emerging on to a golf course. Turn right, along the edge of the wood. Go through a gate and continue. Bear left through a gate and then right to follow the edge of the woods, downhill. Go through a gate and bear right again, down the fence to a bridge and up to a gate on the right. Go through into the woods and bear left, soon leaving via a gate. Follow this path down the field towards **Hermitage**. Go through a gate, cross a stream and turn right up to the church, Point Ⓓ. Here art treasures from Bournemouth were hung for protection during the Second World War.

Retrace your steps to the gate. Go through and bear right, to turn right under a tree. Go through another gate and keep straight on. Now go through a further gate and bear left. At the top corner cross a stile and follow the hedge to the right. Cross two stiles and walk up the field towards **Lyon's Hill Farm**. Take the gate on the right, to walk straight on, up the drive, until you reach a road. Turn left, descending to the main road. Cross over and go straight ahead up the gravel track. Pass a radio mast on your right. Directly above **Minterne House**, rejoin Walk 43 at Point ⑥.

Walk 45

The Three Melburies

Link two attractive villages and an eccentric mansion.

•DISTANCE•	6 miles (9.7km)
•MINIMUM TIME•	3hrs
•ASCENT / GRADIENT•	656ft (200m) ▲▲▲
•LEVEL OF DIFFICULTY•	🚶🚶 🚶🚶 🚶
•PATHS•	Village lanes, estate tracks, farmland paths, 10 stiles
•LANDSCAPE•	Hills, valleys and parkland
•SUGGESTED MAP•	aqua3 OS Explorer 117 Cerne Abbas & Bere Regis
•START / FINISH•	Grid reference: ST 573077
•DOG FRIENDLINESS•	Fun may be limited by lots of notices to keep dogs on leads; some lifting over stiles may be necessary
•PARKING•	By church, Melbury Osmond, signed off A37
•PUBLIC TOILETS•	None on route

Walk 45 Directions

Walk down the street through this lovely village of thatched houses. Cross the watersplash at the bottom via the pavement and packhorse bridge. Pass the **Old Chapel** on the right and **Townsend Dairy House** then continue up the road. Cross a stile by a cattle grid and take the straight estate road down a newly planted avenue of trees. Follow this for almost a mile (1.6km) to **Melbury House** (private), which is part of the Ilchester Estate. The famous glazed tower, with windows all round the upper level, pokes above a roof punctuated by tall chimney stacks and pointed gables.

Turn right along the road just before the house and follow it round the outbuildings and left through a gate. Look out for the fallow deer, for whom the gates and fences were built. Continue on this road for another ¾ mile (1.2km) through the park, up and over a hill. Cross a stile by a gateway. With

Evershot in sight ahead, hook back up to the left on a bridleway, passing a house on the right. Follow this up the hill. Where it divides, keep straight ahead downhill. Pass a plantation on the right. At a junction near the bottom turn right. Follow the track as it curves left and starts to rise. Where the wood on your right runs out, bear left up the field, towards a small gate. Go through this and follow the path ahead and left through a young plantation, to the **A37** by a milestone. Cross over with care and take the bridleway ahead.

Go through the gate and turn left through another gate. Follow the field edge round to the right below the woods. In the far corner turn right through a gate and bear left down the track through woodland. At the other side go through a gate and straight ahead over the field, keeping right of the trig point, and turning right along the hedge. Go through a gate and turn down towards **Melbury Bubb**. Use two gates to go through a farmyard,

Walk 45

passing a wooden granary on staddle stones to the left.

Follow the lane right to explore the church. It has a barrel roof, fragments of old glass and some good windows, and is heated by a wood-burning stove and lit by oil lamps. Look for the font to the left of the door, it's strongly carved with deer, hounds and other beasts intertwined with foliage. Oddly, it's upside down and tapers the wrong way – it is believed to be part of a recycled 11th-century Anglo-Saxon cross, hollowed out at one end to make a font, and shows creatures from the Bestiary laden with Christian symbolism.

Retrace your route back up to the trig point, passing it on the left this time. Bear diagonally left down over the field from here, passing above two steep combes. Bear right to cross a stile in the far corner. Walk along duckboards through boggy woodland, cross a stile into a field and bear left, joining a gravel farm track. Pass **Church Farm** to the left. Beside it is **St Edwold's Church**, the second smallest church in England (with an outsize belfry).

Bear right up the farm road. At the top turn right, and soon left, through a gate into a field by a fingerpost. Turn right and walk along the hedge. Cross a stile and bear left down the next field. About half-way down bear left through a gate (yellow marker) and continue right along this line, meeting a hedge at a corner. Ignore a bridge down to the right and continue diagonally left to the far end of the field, to cross a stile, footbridge and another stile. Head diagonally left across the next field, to emerge through a gate on to the **A37** beside the **Rest And Welcome Inn**.

Turn left and walk along the verge. Cross with care, to take the footpath over a stile just before a car sales yard. Follow this straight ahead down the hedge. Go through a gate and turn left to cross a stile, footbridge and a further stile. Go straight across the field towards a stone house. Bear left through the gate and walk on to the road by the watersplash. Turn right to return to the church.

The Monarch's Way Through Winyard's Gap

In Dorset's northern uplands, a short circular walk follows the route of an historic royal escape.

•DISTANCE•	3¼ miles (5.3km)
•MINIMUM TIME•	1hr 30min
•ASCENT / GRADIENT•	410ft (125m) ▲▲▲
•LEVEL OF DIFFICULTY•	林 林 林
•PATHS•	Field paths, some roads, 1 stile
•LANDSCAPE•	Little hills and valleys around high ridge
•SUGGESTED MAP•	aqua3 OS Explorer 117 Cerne Abbas & Bere Regis
•START / FINISH•	Grid reference: ST 491060
•DOG FRIENDLINESS•	Generally good but some road walking a bit tiring
•PARKING•	Lay-by north of Cheddington, opposite Court Farm
•PUBLIC TOILETS•	None on route

BACKGROUND TO THE WALK

In 1651 the rightful claimant to the English throne found himself on the run in Dorset. The young Charles II had been making for the coast, but was chased back inland. Forced to take a longer route via Yeovil and Mottisfont, he eventually reached Shoreham, where he could catch a ship to exile on the Continent.

Charles had an unfortunate inheritance. His father, Charles I, was the first and only British monarch to be executed, after a long and divisive struggle against his own Parliament. As Prince of Wales, the young Charles had fought in early battles of the Civil War, but had been packed off to Europe when it became clear that things might not go the King's way. (Part of his exile was spent in Jersey, where his illegitimate son James, Duke of Monmouth, was born, ► Walk 3.) Charles was only 19 years old when his father died on the scaffold in 1649.

Worcester Force

The Scots promptly proclaimed the young prince King, and invited him home. On 1 January 1651 he was duly crowned Charles II at Scone Palace. However, the English Parliament was not going to give up its grip that easily. At the Battle of Worcester in September of that year, Cromwell's army triumphed, and Charles had to flee for his life. The Worcester defeat effectively marked the end of the Civil War. It was to be another nine years before the mood of the country changed and the 'Merry Monarch' could be invited back to take up his throne.

Bedroom Farce

From Worcester the young Charles fled south through the Cotswolds, reaching the home of the Wyndham family at Trent, on the north Dorset border, where he went into hiding. From here a ship was arranged to take him to France. The King was to rendezvous with the skipper, Stephen Limbry, at the Queens Head pub in Charmouth, disguised as the servant to an eloping couple. Things did not go to plan. Charles was a wanted man and his description had been widely posted. Limbry's wife became suspicious and, fearing that her husband might be captured himself, locked him in his bedroom. When the captain failed to show up, Charles moved boldly on to Bridport, but only escaped from there by a whisker. He made his way back to the Wyndhams via Broadwindsor and holed up for another 12 days, before a second attempt to reach a ship and safety was successful.

Today the route of Charles II's flight is commemorated with a long distance path called the Monarch's Way, which leads through the narrow defile in the high ridge called Winyard's Gap. It is ironic that his father had come the same way at the head of an army and in a much more bombastic mood, seven years earlier whilst campaigning in Dorset.

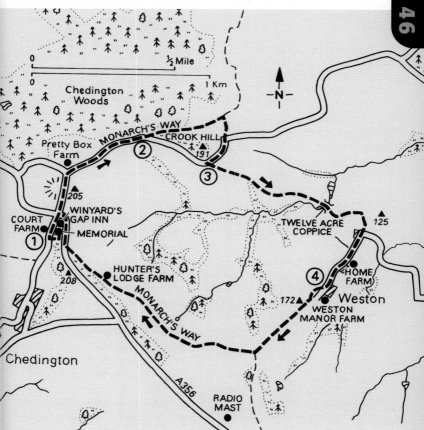

Walk 46 Directions

① Go through the gate at the back of the lay-by and bear right on the path up through the woods. At the top of the ridge turn left for the memorial. Turn left down the steps, go back through the gate and turn

right along the road. Pass the **Winyard's Gap Inn** on the right then, at the junction, cross straight over and walk up the road ahead. Sweeping views open out to the west. Keep right, following the lane over the top of the ridge between shoulder-high banks – the sign of an ancient lane. Flat-topped,

Walk 46

bracken-clad Crook Hill is ahead. After about ½ mile (800m) bear left through a gate, signposted 'Monarch's Way'.

② Bear right along the top of the field, with **Chedington Woods** falling steeply away on the left, and Crook Hill ahead and right. Go through a gate at the foot of the hill and bear right through the woods, round the base. Cross a stile and bear left down the field. On reaching a farm road near some trees, turn right. Follow it up to meet a lane and turn right.

③ After a short distance, on a corner, go left through a gate and hook back down the fence on the bridleway. Go through two gates at the bottom and continue down the field, parallel with the top hedge. **Twelve Acre Coppice**, down to the right, is a lovely stretch of mixed woodland. At the bottom cross the stream via a bridge, then go

through the gate and straight ahead up the track. Go through a gate to the left of a barn (indicated by a blue marker) and turn right on the farm road, through a farmyard. At the lane go straight ahead, passing **Home Farm** on the left, into the hamlet of **Weston**.

④ Just before **Weston Manor Farm** detour right through a gate (blue marker). Turn left through a gate and turn right to resume the track straight up the hill, with a radio mast topping the ridge ahead. After a short tunnel of trees bear right through a gate along a green track, part of the **Monarch's Way**. Go through a gate and stay on the track. Go through another gate with ponds down to the right. Soon pass through a second gate to the left of a barn, walk past **Hunter's Lodge Farm** and up the drive to the road. Turn right on the main road and follow it back down to the inn, with care. Turn left here to return to the lay-by and your car.

Forde Abbey and the Valley of the Axe

You'll find the going is fairly easy on this tranquil circuit through an area renowned for its soft fruit.

Walk 47

•DISTANCE•	5 miles (8km)
•MINIMUM TIME•	2hrs 30min
•ASCENT / GRADIENT•	443ft (135m) ▲▲ ▲
•LEVEL OF DIFFICULTY•	🏃🏃 🏃🏃 🏃🏃
•PATHS•	Field paths, country lanes, 18 stiles
•LANDSCAPE•	Tranquil, broad, fertile valley
•SUGGESTED MAP•	aqua3 OS Explorer 116 Lyme Regis & Bridport
•START / FINISH•	Grid reference: ST 373029
•DOG FRIENDLINESS•	Keep on lead along roads
•PARKING•	At crossroads south west of Thorncombe
•PUBLIC TOILETS•	None on route

BACKGROUND TO THE WALK

To reach Thorncombe you must travel on some of the narrowest lanes in Dorset, it seems. Go slowly, for visibility is limited to the next bend and you don't want to miss anything. Signposting is erratic and you could almost believe that few visitors have penetrated this charming quarter in the last 100 years. You'd be mistaken, for a famous gem on the Dorset heritage trail lies this way.

Edmund Prideaux

Buried deep in rolling green countryside on a bend of the River Axe, the majestic buildings of Forde Abbey today ooze charm and contentment. It is difficult to imagine them lying abandoned for almost a century yet, after the Cistercian monastery that had occupied the site for some 400 years was closed down in 1539, that is exactly what happened. The spell was broken by a new purchaser in 1649, Edmund Prideaux, who had risen to a position of power during the Civil War. His career peaked shortly after as Attorney General to Oliver Cromwell. Prideaux's reputation was severely damaged, however, when it was revealed that his son had entertained the rebel Duke of Monmouth here in 1680, and a hefty fine for suspected sympathies after Monmouth's defeat at Sedgemoor (➤ Walk 3) was to cripple him financially. In his early, buoyant years at Forde, Prideaux made his own modifications to a structure that was already rather splendid, thanks to the work of a previous incumbent, the abbot Thomas Chard. The initials 'T C' may be seen on the oriel windows of the great, square entrance tower. Prideaux's priority was to make a family home, so he shortened the Great Hall, turned the chapter house into a private chapel and remodelled the monks' gallery into a saloon, among other improvements. The beautiful, garlanded plasterwork ceilings date from this time.

Vivid Mortlake tapestries depicting the *Acts of the Apostles* which hang in the saloon were an addition in the next century, presented by Queen Anne to her Secretary of War, Sir Francis Gwyn, who had come into ownership of the estate by marriage.

Exemplary Abbey

While the house is fascinating, it is the setting of the abbey within the gardens which is most memorable. Photos of the house invariably show the beautiful planting at the front, viewed from across the still waters of the Long Pond, with neatly clipped specimen yews and deep beds of summer flowers. It's open all year and truly a garden for all seasons, with a kitchen garden, stunning herbaceous borders, a rock garden (created from old gravel workings), a bog garden, an arboretum for autumn colour and drifts of snowdrops lining the approach in early spring. Dog owners will be pleased to hear that, providing they are kept on a short lead, dogs are actually welcome here.

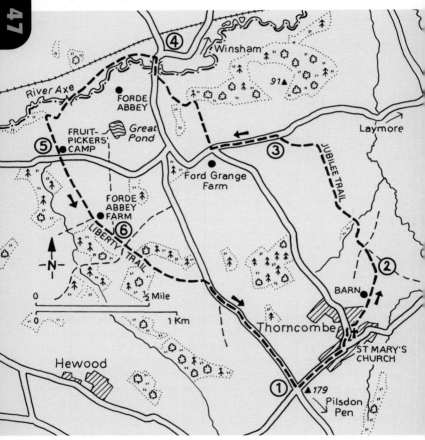

Walk 47 Directions

① Turn left (north east) and walk down into **Thorncombe**. Turn left up **Chard Street** and take the footpath on the right through the churchyard. Bear right down the lane and soon left on a gravel track

beside a wall, opposite **Goose Cottage**. Cross a stile into a field, pass a barn on the left, then go straight on down the hedge.

② Cross a stile in the corner and go straight across the field. Cross a stile and bear diagonally right, down to the corner of the next field. Cross a stile, then a second stile on the right. Ford the stream and bear left, up the field. Cross a stile on the left, and continue up. Soon cross another stile on the right, then bear right round the edge of the field. The track veers right through the hedge. Cross two more stiles and continue straight on. By a trough turn left over a pair of stiles and go straight ahead up the field edge. Go through a gate and bear right, towards a house.

> **WHAT TO LOOK FOR** ⓘ
>
> Look into **St Mary's Church** at Thorncombe for a sight of two splendid 15th-century brasses, memorials to Sir Thomas and Lady Joan Brook. Standing over 5ft (1.5m) high, they depict the pair in the flowing dress of the period, their feet resting on pet dogs.

③ Emerge through a gate on to a road and turn left. At the junction turn right on to a path and head straight for the woods. Turn left before the edge of the woods and, at the corner go right, through a gate. Head diagonally left to the bottom corner, opposite the gates of **Forde Abbey**. Cross a stile and turn right on the road to cross the **River Axe**.

④ Turn immediately left on to the footpath and follow it round past the back of the Abbey. At the far corner cross a footbridge over the river and bear right towards a lone

> **WHERE TO EAT AND DRINK** ⓘ
>
> There are attractive tea rooms at **Forde Abbey**, but if you're looking for something more substantial, head for the **Squirrel Inn** at nearby Laymore. It offers real ales, imaginative and top-notch home-cooking, freshly made sandwiches and a family room. Outside there's a beer garden and a good-sized children's play area. Dogs are welcome.

> **WHILE YOU'RE THERE** ⓘ
>
> The boast of **Pilsdon Pen** is that, at 909ft (277m), it is the highest hill in Dorset. It lies to the south east of Thorncombe and is topped by an ancient fort. There are extensive views south over the Marshwood Vale towards Golden Cap and the sea. William Wordsworth and his sister Dorothy lived for a time at nearby Racedown, and climbed the hill regularly.

cedar, then bear left up the slope to a stile, marked 'Liberty Trail'. Cross this, then walk along the top of the woods. Soon cross a stile and bear left across the fields towards another giant cedar.

⑤ Meet the road by a fruit-pickers' camp. Go straight across, through a gate and straight up the field. Towards the top right-hand corner bear right through a gate, then keep on this line. Cross a pair of stiles in the corner, pass **Forde Abbey Farm** on the left and keep straight on by the hedge. Cross a stile and walk down the track.

⑥ At a junction of tracks keep straight on. Where the track forks bear left, go through a gate and bear left across the field. Cross a stile in the hedge and turn right up the road. Stay on this for ½ mile (800m) to return to your car.

Golden Cap in Trust

Climb a fine top, owned by one of the country's most popular charities.

•DISTANCE•	4 miles (6.4km)
•MINIMUM TIME•	2hrs 30min
•ASCENT / GRADIENT•	1,007ft (307m) ▲▲▲
•LEVEL OF DIFFICULTY•	👥 👥 👥
•PATHS•	Field tracks, country lanes, steep zig-zag gravel path, 7 stiles
•LANDSCAPE•	Windswept coastline of lumps and bumps
•SUGGESTED MAP•	aqua3 OS Explorer 116 Lyme Regis & Bridport
•START / FINISH•	Grid reference: SY 420917
•DOG FRIENDLINESS•	Some road walking
•PARKING•	Car park (charge) above gravel beach in Seatown; beware, can flood in stormy weather
•PUBLIC TOILETS•	At end of road, Seatown

BACKGROUND TO THE WALK

Golden Cap is the rather obvious name for a high, flat-topped hill of deep orange sandstone on the cliffs between Charmouth and Bridport. It represents the tail end of a vein of the warm-coloured sandstone that stretches down from the Cotswolds. The Cap is the highest point on the south coast, at 627ft (191m), with views along the shore to the tip of Portland Bill in one direction and to Start Point in the other. Inland, you can see Pilsdon Pen and as far as the heights of Dartmoor.

Important Habitat

Climbing towards the top, you pass from neat fields, through a line of wind-scoured oak trees, into an area of high heathland, walking up through bracken, heather, bilberry and blackberry, alive with songbirds. The loose undercliff on the seaward side creates a different habitat. In botanical and wildlife terms, Golden Cap is one of the richest properties in the National Trust's portfolio. Today we tend to associate the National Trust with the upkeep of grand houses but, in fact, its first acquisition, way back in 1896, was a stretch of coast in Wales. Today the charity is one of Britain's biggest private landowners.

Earl of Antrim

On the very top of Golden Cap itself is a simple memorial to the Earl of Antrim, chairman of the Trust in the 1960s and 1970s. It was he who spearheaded its 1965 appeal campaign, named 'Enterprise Neptune', to purchase sections of unspoiled coastline before the developers moved in and it was all too late. Golden Cap was part of this and over the years the Trust has continued to buy up pockets of land all around, with the aim of preserving the traditional field pattern that exists in the area between Eype and Lyme Regis.

Its acquisition includes the ruined church of St Gabriel's (little more than a low shell with a porch to one side) and the neighbouring row of thatched cottages that have been smartly refurbished and are let out as visitor accommodation. They are all that remains of the fishing village of Stanton, sheltering in the valley behind the cliffs, which was largely abandoned after the coast road was rerouted inland in 1824.

Walk 49 continues inland to Morcombelake, and finally back over Langdon Hill, also owned by the National Trust. Seen from the speedy A35 coast road, Morcombelake is an unexciting ribbon development, to be hurried through on your way to somewhere else. On foot, however, you discover a network of narrow, winding lanes on the slopes of Langdon Hill that takes you into a different, tranquil world. Rambling houses with old bay windows have a confident, nautical air, as though this was a place for retired admirals.

Walk 48 Directions

① Walk back up through **Seatown**. Cross a stile on the left, on to the footpath, signposted 'Coast Path

Diversion'. Cross a stile at the end, bear left to cross a stile and footbridge into woodland. Cross a pair of stiles at the other side and bear right up the hill, signposted 'Golden Cap'.

Walk 48

② Where the track forks keep left. Go through some trees and over a stile. Bear left, straight across the open hillside, with Golden Cap ahead of you. Pass through a line of trees and walk up the fence. Go up some steps, cross a stile and continue ahead. At the fingerpost go left through a gate to follow the path of shallow steps up through bracken, heather, bilberry and bramble to the top of **Golden Cap**.

WHERE TO EAT AND DRINK ⓘ
The **Anchor Inn** at Seatown promises an interesting selection of ales, food and wine. The terrace overlooking the beach fills up quickly in summer. The rusted anchor outside belonged to the *Hope*, which was wrecked on Chesil Beach during a storm in January 1748, while returning from Curaçao to Amsterdam. The crew escaped to safety on the beach, but the ship broke up, shedding £50,000 worth of gold, silver and other valuables, creating a mini gold-rush.

③ Pass the trig point and turn right along the top. Pass the **stone memorial** to the Earl of Antrim. At a marker stone turn right and follow the zig-zag path steeply downhill, enjoying great views along the bay to Charmouth and Lyme Regis. Go through a gate and bear right over the field towards the ruined **St Gabriel's Church**. In the bottom corner turn down through

WHILE YOU'RE THERE ⓘ
The quay at **West Bay** in Bridport, was the setting for the *Harbour Lights* television drama series. It has the genuine, slightly seedy air of a working harbour and remains refreshingly unsophisticated. The harbour has a long, very narrow entrance and water surges through in a storm. Eat fish and chips from a kiosk while you admire the fishing boats and other craft.

WHAT TO LOOK FOR ⓘ
Moore's biscuit bakery in Morcombelake is a fascinating detour, worth it for the smell alone. Through a glass screen see the biscuits being hand-made – and sample as you watch. There's also a gallery of artwork associated with its packaging. The famous savoury Dorset knobs, thrice-baked and explosively crisp, are a post-Christmas speciality. Open weekdays, and Saturday mornings in summer.

a gate, passing the ruins on your right, then go through a second gate. Go down the track, passing cottages on the left, and bear right up the road, signed 'Morcombelake'. Follow this up between high banks and hedges which put the wild flowers conveniently at eye-level. Continue through a gateway.

④ At the road junction, turn right down **Muddyford Lane**, signed 'Langdon Hill' (or go straight on for Walk 49). Pass the gate of **Shedbush Farm** (Walk 49 rejoins) and continue straight up the hill. Turn right up a concreted lane towards **Filcombe Farm**. Follow blue markers through the farmyard, bearing left through two gates. Walk up the track, go through two more gates and bear left over the top of the green saddle between Langdon Hill and Golden Cap.

⑤ Go left through a gate in the corner and down a gravel lane (**Pettycrate Lane**) beside the woods, signed 'Seatown'. Ignore a footpath off to the right. At a junction of tracks keep right, downhill, with a delectable green patchwork of fields on the hillside ahead. Pass **Seahill House** on the left and turn right, on to a road. Continue down the road into Seatown village to return to your car.

Morcombelake Loop

Take this extension to embrace the breezy heath on Hardown Hill.
See map and information panel for Walk 48

•DISTANCE•	6½ miles (10.4km)
•MINIMUM TIME•	3hrs 45min
•ASCENT / GRADIENT•	1,332ft (406m) ▲▲▲
•LEVEL OF DIFFICULTY•	👫 👫 👫

Walk 49 Directions
(Walk 48 option)

At Point ④ on Walk 48 go straight ahead, on to the broad track and follow it up the valley, with Chardown and Stonebarrow hills up to the left. A former radar station on Stonebarrow Hill has been adapted to accommodate the National Trust's volunteer working parties. There is also an information point and shop during summer (access by road from Charmouth). Pass **Cold Harbour House** on the right. Go through two gates. At a road bear right and keep right, past **Ship Farm** to the **A35**, Point Ⓐ.

Cross with care and turn left at the **Ship Inn**. Take the first road right up the hill, signposted 'Whitchurch Canonicorum'. Almost immediately turn right and bear left up **Pitmans Lane**. This narrow road wraps itself around the hilltop, offering glimpses into the appealing nooks and crannies of Morcombelake. There are extensive views down to the left of little green hills and scattered Whitchurch Canonicorum, dominated by its impressive church. Look left by **Pitmans House** for a clear view down to Charmouth. Carry straight on as **Taylors Lane** feeds in from the left, leaving the houses behind for the wilder tops. At a gate bear right, up a footpath by a fingerpost, towards the heath. After rising, this leads round the back of the hill into a quiet green world with lovely views over the valley. Look for the crossing of a deep-cut path – turn right, up this. Bear right at the top, up the track. Turn left by the National Trust sign and follow this broad track, up over the top of the exposed heath on **Hardown Hill**. Pass a bench on the left, then follow the track round and down, to emerge at a road junction. Turn left and walk down **Gibbs Lane** to meet the **A35** near Morcombelake's post office, Point Ⓑ.

Cross and turn left. **Moore's** renowned biscuit shop is just ahead, but turn off to the right before it, down **Shedbush Lane**. You'll pass the replacement **St Gabriel's Church**, built in 1841, on the left. At the bottom of the lane cross a stile and bear right along the field edge. Continue down to a gate and bear left through **Shedbush Farm**, a splendid brick and thatch affair (with Tamworth pigs in the open barns when I last passed). Follow the farm drive down to the road and turn left, rejoining Walk 48 on **Muddyford Lane**.

Walk 50

Lyme Regis to Dragon's Hill

A walk in the hills behind the town that ends on the famous Cobb.

•DISTANCE•	4 miles (6.4km)
•MINIMUM TIME•	2hrs
•ASCENT / GRADIENT•	427ft (130m) ▲▲▲
•LEVEL OF DIFFICULTY•	👥 👥 👥
•PATHS•	Town centre, promenade, woodland steps, paths, 1 stile
•LANDSCAPE•	Town, cliffs and hinterland of steep valley
•SUGGESTED MAP•	aqua3 OS Explorer 116 Lyme Regis & Bridport
•START / FINISH•	Grid reference: SY 337916
•DOG FRIENDLINESS•	Very busy in summer, dogs banned from shingle beach
•PARKING•	Pay-and-display near Cobb (other car parks on route)
•PUBLIC TOILETS•	Signposted at several car parks and seafront

Walk 50 Directions

From the harbour car park, face inland and take the path to the left of the bowling green, up some steps between wooden chalets, signed 'Coastal Path'. Cross a road and continue via more steps up through steep woodland, beside a stream. Cross a stile at the top and turn right. Go through a gate and continue along a path and then a road between villas, to cross a car park. Cross the road ahead and, with **Coram Tower** on your left, go straight on down **Pound Road**. Pass the thatched **Cursbrook Hotel**. Meet the **B3165** opposite the **Mariners Hotel**. Cross this then go down **Woodmead Road**. Soon turn left through a gate and follow the path down through a plantation.

Go through a gate on to **Roman Road**. Bear right, cross the **River Lim** and turn left down a lane. By **Middle Mill Farm** cross a footbridge. Continue along the valley floor. At the corner bear right

through a gate, cross a footbridge and bear right at the fork. Pass a thatched cottage on the left and turn right over a bridge (blue marker). Follow this path through woods to a gate. Continue past the sewage works and through another gate into a field.

Go straight on up the hill, with **Sleech Wood** to your left. Continue through a gate. Near the top of **Dragon's Hill** go through a gate and turn right, down a lane. Stay on this below a caravan park to emerge on **Charmouth Road**. Turn right and follow this for ½ mile (800m), down into the town, taking care where the pavement runs out. Pass the former **London** pub (now a B&B) and enter the old town. Turn

> **WHILE YOU'RE THERE** ⓘ
> For something different, go to sea. **Deep-sea fishing** trips are offered from Lyme and lots of little boats are available for charter. They advertise a variety of adventures and expeditions on the seafront near the Cobb. There's mackerel fishing in season, too.

right into **Monmouth Street**, passing through a delightful square with gardens. Keep right, up the hill, towards Dinosaurland. Pass **Dinosaurland** on the right, with a fossil museum and shop. Continue uphill. Take the riverside path on the left, signposted 'Town Mill'. The stream is on your left, the river below to your right.

WHERE TO EAT AND DRINK ℹ

In Lyme the smart **Millside Coffee Shop and Wine Bar** is beside the old Town Mill. Lunch options include grilled red snapper and Thai curry. The traditional **Royal Standard** pub, in a harbour setting near the Cobb, offers local fish dishes, from scallops served with garlic toast to crabs and lobster. There's a beer garden on the seaward side. Dogs are welcome on a lead.

Turn left up **Mill Lane,** and right on to **Coombe Street**, towards the harbour. Here you get the impression of lots of tiny houses tightly packed together. Bear left at the end, by the Lyme Fossil Shop, on to **Broad Street**, towards the tourist information centre. Turn right by the Guildhall, and right again along the sea, via the fortifications, **Guncliffe Walk**, really a disguise for a new sewage scheme.

Pass a huge anchor and bear right up **Broad Street**, as far as the **Royal Lion Hotel**. Walk down the opposite pavement, around the old shambles, to **Bell Cliff**. Go down the steps and turn right along **Marine Parade**. Local philanthropist Thomas Hollis created this walkway in 1771 as an alternative to the lower cart road. Shingle on your left gives way to sand near the amusement arcades. The buildings on the eastern arm of the harbour now house an aquarium. Continue up a lane, passing the **Royal Standard** on your left. Bear left by the **Cobb Arms** and walk down to the end of the **Cobb**.

The Cobb is a breakwater, first constructed in the 13th century to protect the town from the sea. The sheltered harbour it created made Lyme Dorset's second largest port. The Cobb was rebuilt in Portland stone in the early 19th century with a walkway on the sheltered side. While the shipping trade had waned by then, cargoes were still being unloaded here into the 20th century. Jane Austen visited Lyme Regis in 1804, and set a pivotal scene of her novel *Persuasion* (1818) on the Cobb – the impetuous Louisa Musgrove mistimed her jump from the steps. (The house where Jane Austen stayed was recently pulled down and replaced by a memorial garden, above Marine Parade.) The Cobb gained contemporary fame when scenes for the 1981 film, *The French Lieutenant's Woman*, were shot here. It was based on the novel by John Fowles who was curator of the local history museum for many years.

Return, turning left by the **Lifeboat Station** to get back to the car park.

WHAT TO LOOK FOR ℹ

In 1811, in the cliffs near the town, Mary Anning discovered the first complete icthyosaurus – a marine reptile a bit like a dolphin, which grew up to 33ft (10m) long. It's now the pride of London's Natural History Museum. **Dinosaurland** is a fascinating fossil museum, with icthyosaurs, plesiosaurs and other Jurassic delights, plus a time gallery to show what life was like 4.6 billion years ago. Take your own finds to its fossil clinic, or go with an expert guide on a fossil walk.

Walking in Safety

All these walks are suitable for any reasonably fit person, but less experienced walkers should try the easier walks first. Route finding is usually straightforward, but you will find that an Ordnance Survey map is a useful addition to the route maps and descriptions.

Risks

Although each walk here has been researched with a view to minimising the risks to the walkers who follow its route, no walk in the countryside can be considered to be completely free from risk. Walking in the outdoors will always require a degree of common sense and judgement to ensure that it is as safe as possible.

- Be particularly careful on cliff paths and in upland terrain, where the consequences of a slip can be very serious.

- Remember to check tidal conditions before walking on the seashore.

- Some sections of route are by, or cross, busy roads. Take care and remember traffic is a danger even on minor country lanes.

- Be careful around farmyard machinery and livestock, especially if you have children with you.

- Be aware of the consequences of changes in the weather and check the forecast before you set out. Carry spare clothing and a torch if you are walking in the winter months. Remember the weather can change very quickly at any time of the year, and in moorland and heathland areas, mist and fog can make route finding much harder. Don't set out in these conditions unless you are confident of your navigation skills in poor visibility. In summer remember to take account of the heat and sun; wear a hat and carry spare water.

- On walks away from centres of population you should carry a whistle and survival bag. If you do have an accident requiring the emergency services, make a note of your position as accurately as possible and dial 999.

Acknowledgements

The author would like to thank Chris Bagshaw at Outcrop Publishing Services and Sandy Breakwell at AA Publishing for the opportunity to get to know Dorset; the fellow walkers who put me on the right track when lost; the helpful locals and landowners who suggested better routes; Tourist Information staff across the county; Heather and Michael French, who lent me their complete archive of the *Dorset Magazine*, an invaluable source of inspiration and information; Caroline Adamyk, who came to Cerne; and Skipper and Freya, four-legged walking companions who shared the highs, the lows and the sandwiches.

AA Publishing and Outcrop Publishing Services would like to thank Chartech for supplying aqua3 maps for this book. For more information visit their website: www.aqua3.com.

Series management: Outcrop Publishing Services Ltd, Cumbria
Series editor: Chris Bagshaw
Front cover: AA Photo Library/Peter Baker